How to Create a
MAGICAL
College Life

25 Strategies for Better Grades,
Healthier Relationships, and
Super Self-Confidence!

How to Create a
MAGICAL
College Life

25 Strategies for Better Grades,
Healthier Relationships, and
Super Self-Confidence!

Morris Taylor

Talisman Training Associates, LLC
Round Lake Beach, Illinois

Published by
Talisman Training Associates, LLC
P.O. Box 524, Round Lake Beach, IL 60073

Interior book design and typesetting by JustYourType.biz

Library of Congress Control Number: 2006900232

ISBN: 0-9779219-0-5

Printed in the United States of America

CONTENTS

INTRODUCTION:
Standing at the Crossroad

This is the book I wish I'd had when I was starting college. It's a book that focuses on how to get the kinds of results that will serve you well, both now and in the future (i.e., following graduation), as you enter into your career, marriage, various business and personal relationships, etc. In other words, it is a book that will help you be successful in *all phases of your life*.

I know that's a tall order. I also know that books that make these kinds of claims are a dime a dozen, and most of them are written in a way that lets you know right away that the author either doesn't really know what he or she is talking about, or is woefully out of touch with the fast-paced, frenetic, and multi-faceted lifestyle that many teenagers live.

You will find that this book is different. First of all, you can see this is not a thick book. It's relatively small. The reason for this is that I'm a lot like you. I'm busy, you're busy. If you're in college, you don't have time for another thick book. I made it short because I want you to finish it. It will take you less than a couple of hours. During that time, give these pages your full attention and you'll be better for it — I promise.

Secondly, the premise is a little different. In my lectures and presentations, I use magic, specifically *mentalism,* as a metaphor. Mentalism (i.e., the use of ESP, mind reading, predictions, etc.) is a very special art form. Its very existence demonstrates imaginative thinking. As human beings, we strive to accomplish the impossible, to break through impenetrable barriers and surpass previous limitations.

In one of my stage lectures, I drive this point home by doing a host of things, including a "killer" memory demonstration and *levitating* a member of the audience. No, the levitation is not a trick! We actually do this using a participant from the audience and a group of unprepared volunteers who are simply willing to *suspend their previous notions of what's possible!* And that's the mindset I'd like you to have as you read this book.

At this moment, if you're like most of the readers who pick up this book, you are standing at the crossroad between adolescence and adulthood. As college students, many of you are living on your own for the first time, no longer under the watchful eye of your parents. You're residing in dormitories with other students from a variety of philosophical backgrounds and cultures, with a myriad number of options and choices available to you on any given day. Wow! What a head rush!

But once you get over the initial excitement of this smorgasbord of freedom, you realize that the choices you will make over the next three to four years are critical, because they can potentially impact virtually *every aspect of your life* in the future including where you live, employment options, your future income and financial status, marriage, children, health, and on and on.

Add to this the frustrating fact that at the time you're making those choices, it's almost impossible to know which ones are going to turn out to be the *big* ones and which ones will turn out to be of little consequence. Suddenly, what was once the giddy excitement of new-found freedom is now just one hyperventilated breath away from becoming an anxiety attack!

Philosopher Ashleigh Brilliant once wrote, "Life is the only game in which the object of the game is to learn the rules!" Well, one of the rules I've learned about living a successful life is to learn as much as you can as fast as you can, so that you can leverage your accumulated knowledge and experience to take full advantage of the opportunities that come your way. Which brings us to the purpose of this book.

I often say that success in life is not about being lucky. Success is really dependent on three components: *Preparation, awareness, and opportunity*. You must *prepare* for the outcome you desire, and you must be aware of the environment around you. If you do these first two things, when the *opportunity* arrives, you'll be able to take full advantage of it because you're able to recognize it and you're prepared for it. These three components are really a strategy for achieving success in all of life. Some people still call it being lucky. I call it being *smart!* The purpose of this book is to help you become smart, and the best time to become smart is right here, right now, while you're still *at the crossroad.*

Give me an hour or two. Read this book thoroughly. Make notes in the margins when you need to and highlight the parts you want to reread and consider more thoroughly later. In fact, don't hesitate to read the entire book more than once; it's short but there's a lot here if you'll think about these strategies and take them to heart. They aren't just the keys to a magical *college* life. Practice them now, while you still have relative freedom from responsibility (you lucky dog!), and you'll find that you will not only get the most out of your college years, you'll also get the most out of your entire life!

To your success,
Morris Taylor

PART 1:
Your Mindset

The Internal thoughts and attitudes that create a magical college life

Strategy # 1
Know your college imperative

An imperative is an unavoidable fact, need or obligation;
something that demands immediate attention;
something that has the power to restrain, control,
or direct your actions or decisions.

Why do you want to go to college? Why do you want a college degree? What are you willing to do, to sacrifice, to "put up with" in order to do well and graduate on schedule?

If you're like most people, you probably found the first question to be relatively simple, but each of the subsequent questions become more complex and require more introspection in order to answer. That's because most people entering college never think about the reasons behind their decision in quite this way. Worse still is the fact that even though most people have a reason for going to college, it isn't always *their* reason.

For example, some high school graduates go to college because their parents think they should. Others go because their friends are going. Some go because they don't know what else to do, or they want to find a spouse, etc. The problem with these reasons is that they aren't the kinds of reasons that will push you to persevere when things get tough. And at some point in your college career, things *will* get tough! You will be pushed beyond your current capacities, and you will have to reach down deep into yourself to find the "stuff" necessary to make it through to the other side. I'm not saying this to scare you; it's just to say that college, under the best of circumstances, is almost never easy, and for some it can be flat out hard! So how do you put the odds in your favor? You simply learn ahead of time what to expect, and prepare yourself to deal with it (which, by the way, is the point of this book).

The key lesson here is that in order to succeed in college, you have to have a good reason to succeed, and it has to be *your* reason, not someone else's. I call it your "college imperative." For example, if you've ever tried to quit smoking or lose weight, you know that you can't do it because your doctor or your parents said you should do it. You have to want to do it for yourself. Otherwise, when you feel that nicotine craving or you see that dessert tray at your favorite restaurant, other people's opinions about how you should live your life aren't going to be enough to keep you from giving in to temptation.

Only if you have the conviction that comes from a personal desire and commitment will you find the strength to succeed. College is like that. There are so many ways you can backslide, so many temptations you can give in to, so many opportunities to make choices that are not in the best interest of your college education. If you don't have a *red-hot imperative* to hold on tight and "do the right thing," you just aren't going to make it. Period.

How to benefit from this strategy

To help you identify your college imperative, take out a sheet of paper and answer the following questions. Don't rush through this; take your time and give it some thought. It will be time well spent. And don't forget to answer the last question; that's the one that ties everything together for you.

1. What are the benefits of getting a college degree (i.e., what will you be able to do, be or have if/when you achieve this goal)? To help you think about this question, consider the following:

   How will having a degree impact your

   - self-esteem (how you feel about yourself)?
   - health and fitness (how well you take care of yourself)?
   - communication skills (how clearly you express in words your identity, wants and needs)?
   - relationships (how you interact with the people in your life, whether family, friends, or co-workers)?
   - career/lifework (experiencing challenge, satisfaction, and fulfillment from the work you have chosen)?
   - finances/personal wealth (your ability to manage your money, save, pay your debts, etc.)?
   - pursuit of spiritual enrichment (connecting the physical and emotional aspects of your nature with spiritual awareness)?

2. What will happen if you *don't* get your college degree? What areas of your life will suffer? What life goals do you have that will become more difficult or impossible to achieve?

3. When you consider your strengths and weaknesses and your overall personality, what are the three things most likely to prevent you from being successful in college? What are you prepared to do (or *stop* doing) in order to keep these things from holding you back?

4. What are some of the external obstacles or circumstances that could keep you from being successful in college? How will you overcome these obstacles?

5. Go back and review all of your answers to the above questions. Then complete the following statements.

I am committed to getting a college degree because:

_____

I know I will succeed because:

_____

When circumstances become difficult, I will:

_____

Congratulations — you have just identified your college imperative! Write your college imperative statement on an index card or sheet of paper and post it where you can review it regularly. You may want to revise it periodically, perhaps at the start of each school year, based on your experiences and what you learn about yourself. But always have your college imperative uppermost in your mind and allow it to be your driving force. When nothing seems to be going your way and you begin to wonder if you can make it, meditating on your college imperative will push you to persevere and succeed.

STRATEGY # 2
RESOLVE TO ALWAYS ACCEPT RESPONSIBILITY FOR YOUR CIRCUMSTANCES

We can't always control what happens in our environment or how people treat us, but we can always choose how we respond. We can always choose what happens next!

If you don't digest anything else in this book, if you read only one chapter and set this book down and never pick it up again, STOP RIGHT NOW and focus completely on what I'm about to tell you. If you really listen, understand, and act on this principle, your life will never be the same again. I'm serious. Are you ready?

The following three words are *magic* words:

"I am responsible."

Read these words again: "I am responsible." Now say them out loud: "I AM RESPONSIBLE."

What does this mean? It means from this day forward you resolve not to waste any more time blaming anyone or anything else for what happens in *your* life.

You see, in this world we are surrounded by people who are constantly blaming other people for their life circumstances.

That's the easy way out. Ironically, it is also the habit of most unsuccessful people. In less polite conversation, these people are also called "losers." It's not the fact that they're unsuccessful that makes them losers; it's the fact that they won't accept *personal responsibility* for their lack of success.

I know that's harsh, but we have to face the realities of life if we're going to get better at living it. And the reality is that in order to be successful, you have to take 100 percent responsibility for everything that you experience in your life. Your education, your health and fitness level, your relationships, your career, *everything*.

It's easy to blame others for the parts of our life that we don't like. It's easy because we live in a society in which blaming others has become a common and acceptable practice. We blame our parents, bosses, siblings and friends, astrological chart, biorhythms, the current administration's economic policies, etc. But rarely are we taught to look where the real problem lies, the one problem we have the power to solve — ourselves.

You have to give up all your excuses and take 100 percent responsibility for your future. If you are willing to look honestly at your life, you will realize that you have always had choices. At this point you are still young, so you might argue that in the past you did what you were told by the authority figures in your life and this is how you got where you are. It could also be suggested that you were once too naïve to even realize other options existed. These are valid points, but they don't negate the *principle*. You made a choice. Your choice may have been made out of obedience, ignorance, immaturity, fear, the need to feel safe, be liked or in control, etc., but you made the decision. It's important to understand and accept this principle with all your heart because once you do... you are free!

Let me repeat that. Once you accept responsibility for your life circumstances, YOU ARE FREE! In other words, you become free once you accept that your destiny is not dependent on any other human being; your destiny is entirely in your hands!

You see, although we can't always control what happens in our environment or how people treat us, we can always choose how we respond. We can always choose what happens next. And taking responsibility for that response makes all the difference in the world.

What separates the C+ student from the A+ student? What separates the person who is healthy and fit from the one who is overweight and can't walk up two fights of stairs without pausing to catch his or her breath? What separates the woman who's been in a physically abusive relationship for five years from the one who left her abusive husband/boyfriend after six months?

Choices.

Here's the bottom line. Are you happy with the results you've gotten and are currently getting in your life? If you *are* happy, keep doing what you're doing; in fact, maybe do *more* of it! But if you aren't happy, stop and ask yourself what you need to do differently, what you need to change, what actions you need to take to start getting the results you DO want.

Reprogramming yourself to take personal responsibility

As an exercise, answer the following questions about your own life.

"What could happen to me if I don't:"

❏ Get the education I need to advance my career?

_____

❏ Exercise regularly?

_____

❏ Avoid eating fattening foods?

_____.

❏ End the toxic relationships in my life?

_____.

❏ Choose friends who have high moral and ethical standards?

_____.

❏ Ask my professor(s) for help?

_____.

❏ Develop good study habits?

_____.

❏ Obey the speed limit?

_____.

❏ Stop ignoring my girlfriend/boyfriend?

_____.

❏ Get to my classes on time?

_____.

❏ Learn to manage my time?

_____.

❏ Practice before my next class presentation?

_____.

❏ Earn money over the summer?

_____.

❏ Learn CPR techniques?

_____.

❏ Take my dog to obedience school?

_____.

❏ (Make up your own scenario.)

_____.

Notice that in all of these situations, you are contributing to the undesirable results by the choices you make. Nothing ever just *happens* to you. There is always a cause before there is an effect. If things go wrong later, many people never look back and recognize where they could have had a different outcome if they had made a better choice. Instead, they focus on blaming others, complaining about life, and essentially setting themselves up for the next calamity.

Also notice that there are almost always *warning signs* that you're going down the wrong path. For example, you don't gain 30 extra pounds of body weight overnight; it starts gradually with just a pound or two at a time. You aren't the first person to be unable to help in a situation in which someone needed CPR in order to survive; you've read about such situations, seen them on TV, and have passed over numerous opportunities to enroll in CPR classes. Your dog didn't suddenly become uncontrollable; he increasingly began ignoring your commands and snapping at strangers over a period of months. In each of these situations, when confronted with the warning signs, your decision not to take action contributed to the outcome.

As you begin your college career, remember that you have the power to achieve different, more positive outcomes in your life. To take back the power that is inherently yours, you must accept the truth that you either *create* or *allow* everything that happens in your life. It's always your choice to speak up, make a demand, ask for help, say no, try something new, or walk away. To be successful, you simply have to choose to behave in ways that get the results you want

Don't be like those people who live their lives as if they're bumper cars in a carnival ride, waiting passively for the next collision to send them careening in a new direction. *You* choose the direction. Whatever happens to you, take charge and do what you need to do to make life's circumstances work for you. When you make up your mind to live this way — *really* make up your mind — you will find that the power and energy necessary to create the college life you want is yours to use in whatever way you desire.

How to benefit from this strategy

1. Think back over the last few years of your life. Make a list of some of the things that happened to you that you were not happy about. Then, next to each item, write down the things you did (or failed to do) that directly or indirectly contributed to the undesired outcome(s).

2. Next, make a list of some of the situations you are currently in or that you might conceivably face in the near future. (If you need ideas, look back at the exercise earlier in this chapter.) What actions do you need to take (or avoid) to ensure that you get the outcomes you want?

STRATEGY # 3
REMEMBER, YOUR ATTITUDE DETERMINES
100 PERCENT OF YOUR SUCCESS

Ability is what you're capable of doing. Motivation determines what you do. Attitude determines how well you do it.

— Lou Holtz

Someone showed me this years ago. I thought it was pretty clever.

If you assign a value to each of the 26 letters of the alphabet based on where they fall in the sequence, the values would be as follows:

A = 1

B = 2

C = 3

D = 4

E = 5

Etc.

Using this formula, determine the values for each of the letters in the word ATTITUDE. When you're done, add up the letters for a grand total. What do you get?

The answer is 100. This is a great reminder that ATTITUDE is 100 percent of success! Pretty cute, huh? But it's the truth. When you have the right attitude, almost anything is possible.

Motivational speaker Zig Ziglar often relates the story of the small boy who came home from school and told his father he had to take a math test the following day. "I think I'm going to fail," the boy lamented. "Now, son," said the father, "you have to have a positive attitude." The boy then said, "You're right, dad. I *know* I'm going to fail!" Zig calls that an example of "stinkin' thinking."

The point of the story is that attitude is more about *choice* than *chance*. No one gave you your attitude and no one can take it away from you. It's a choice you make. Have you decided — really *decided* — to succeed in college? That's much stronger and more definite than merely *hoping* you'll succeed! The fact is that successful college students decide to succeed before they even start.

There are numerous examples of people who achieved greatness in the face of tremendous difficulties. Distance runner Roger Bannister did what the doctors and physiologists of the world said was physically and medically impossible when he broke the four-minute mile. He succeeded after countless others before him had tried and failed. Why? *Attitude.*

Sir Edmund Hillary, the first man to successfully climb Mount Everest, finally reached the top of that formidable mountain after numerous personal attempts and after many others had tried and failed, some even dying in the attempt. Why was he able to do it when so many others couldn't? *Attitude.*

Kyle Maynard, the author of *No Excuses,* was born with both arms and legs amputated. Yet he went on to become a star wrestler in college, and today leads a completely normal and active life (even driving a car and typing at a remarkable 50 words per minute!). How did he do it when many others in his situation might easily succumb to such extraordinary limitations? *Attitude.*

In each of these examples, it would be easy to identify the countless reasons why these accomplishments were initially considered by many to be impossible. If you close your eyes, you can almost hear the negative voices of the pessimists:

"No one's done it before."

"All the experts say it can't be done."

"People have died trying to do that."

"How could someone with no hands or fingers learn to type?"

Have you ever asked yourself why some people persevere, never feeling sorry for themselves, never contemplating defeat, always remaining positive and optimistic, and somehow achieve the unexpected, the impossible, the once-in-a-lifetime miracle? It's all *attitude!*

The curious thing about attitude is that it's all in your head — every bit of it. It's never about physical attributes, or financial circumstances, or brains, or luck. If you question this idea, consider the following real world scenario:

Imagine that you're having a terrible day at school. You arrive late for every class. Your friends are all argumentative and everyone seems to be blaming you for something. You missed a project deadline, and you just got back a midterm paper with a grade considerably lower than you expected. By early afternoon your head is starting to hurt, and by the time you get back to your dorm, you have the worst headache you can ever remember. You are absolutely exhausted. You crawl to your bed, sprawl across it, and pull a blanket over your head, totally *whipped.*

Suddenly there's a knock at the door. You reluctantly crawl out of bed to answer it. To your surprise, it's a special guy/girl from your dorm that you've been attracted to for quite a while but who you frankly didn't think even knew you existed. Nonetheless, you've secretly imagined for weeks how great it would be if you could get this person's attention and somehow get them to go out on a date.

And this person says, "I'm sorry to bother you. I don't think we've met but I live here in the building and I just saw you drive up." Before you can respond, the person continues. "My room-mate's sick and needs a prescription filled. Do you think you could give me a ride to the pharmacy and wait with me until it's ready? I'll be happy to buy you dinner on the way home."

So of course you say, "I'm sorry but you're going to have to find somebody else to help you. I've had an *awful* day and I just want to take a hot shower and go to bed!" Right?

Wrong!

What *really* happens at that moment? Suddenly you have a burst of energy! Possibilities are racing through your mind. Excitement is pumping in your veins and you can barely conceal your complete delight!

What changed? Your *attitude!* Where did the change occur? Inside your head, but the change affected your entire body! That's the impact of attitude. The way you *think* about things makes all the difference. That's because of all the communication you do, none is more important than how you talk to yourself. Your internal dialogue has more to do with your ultimate success in life than any other factor.

Let me give you a specific example of how this can apply to your college life. Among the students I've met, both as peers and later as a speaker and facilitator working with students, I've found that there are basically two types.

The first group thinks that when it comes to being smart "either you have it or you don't." Their rationale is, "Some folks are just born with that special *something*. The rest of us have to struggle just to keep our heads above water. Why? It's just the way it is — some people have it and some people don't!"

Then there's the second group. They think, "Smart isn't something you've got. Smart is something you *get!*" Their perspective is, "I may not be the sharpest tack in the box when we start out, but if I mess up, then I know what I need to work on. And from there I can do the work and figure out how to do it right. And pretty soon I'll be performing as well as the best of 'em. Because smart isn't something you're born with, it's something you *become!*"

Which one of these two types of students do you think is more resilient? Which do you think handles setbacks and disappointments better? Which one do you think will be more successful in college and in life? That's right — the second one!

When I studied martial arts we had a saying: "Take the hit as a gift!" In other words, if you are thoroughly beaten in a contest with another student, rather than getting angry or quitting out of embarrassment, the smart student swallows his or her pride and later asks their opponent (or another experienced student or teacher), "What happened? What did he/she do to me? How can I counteract those moves, how can I see those strikes coming, how do I prevent that from happening again?" And that person listens and learns. As a result, the next time they're better prepared. But that only happens because they're able to take the initial defeat (or "hit") as a gift — a gift of awareness. They were shown where they needed to improve, they acted on that information, and as a result they became better.

That's the way you have to be if you're going to have a magical college career. Resolve to learn as much as you can from as many people and other sources as you can. Don't be too proud or stubborn to ask for help. And when things don't go your way, take time to figure out the lessons in your poor performance, and then use that information as your *syllabus* to prepare for the next time.

For example, imagine that you take an exam and when you get back the results you're stunned to see that you didn't do nearly as well as you expected. Now you could say, "That dirty so-and-so professor gave us a test that wasn't fair! She knew we couldn't possibly read all that material in that short amount of time! Why didn't she tell us this would be on the test? And she never liked me anyway!" If you adopt this attitude, you certainly won't be alone!

But instead of wasting time putting the blame on your professor, why not take the opportunity to apply the "monkey see, monkey do" principle (see strategy # 20)? In this particular situation, you could find out who got the highest score in the class (by hook or by crook — even ask the teaching assistant or professor if you have to), and then later approach that person and ask, "How did you study for that test?" Just be friendly and natural and they'll probably tell you quite a bit. Then the next time you have a test in that same class, incorporate their study approach into your own preparation and you'll inevitably improve. *Take the hit as a gift!*

You see, it's not how smart you are when you start out. The student who gets ahead sees the seeds of learning in any poor performance. They see past the immediate disappointment and they take the hit as a gift, because they know that if they apply the lessons learned, that hit can be the best thing that ever happened to them.

When you think about it, this attitude is so logical it should be common sense. But because the initial disappointment, embarrassment, frustration, anger, etc. can be so deep, a lot of people don't see the seeds of their own development right in front of them.

That's why it takes more than logic and common sense.

It takes the right attitude.

How to benefit from this strategy

Answer the following questions:

1. What are some of the hits from your past?

2. Which ones did you benefit from? How did you do it? What did you gain?

3. Which ones did you fail to benefit from? Why? What would you do differently today?

STRATEGY # 4
CREATE A PERSONAL VISION STATEMENT

If you can see it, you can be it.

You hear a lot about vision statements these days, particularly in corporate environments. Many organizations and businesses have vision statements. Unfortunately, most of them rarely (if ever) achieve their visions. The three biggest reasons organizations fail to achieve their visions are the same reasons individuals quite often fail to achieve their personal visions. They are: 1) the vision wasn't specific enough; 2) the organization (i.e., its people) didn't engage in the kinds of day-to-day activities necessary to achieve the vision; and 3) the organization got sidetracked or seduced by other ideas and projects that caused them to lose sight of their vision. If you avoid these three traps, however, a vision of your life after college can be a very powerful tool to keep you focused and on course for a successful college career.

A definition

A personal vision is *a graphic, descriptive picture of some desired future state.* By graphic, I mean that if you were to share

21

it with someone else, the manner in which you articulated it would enable the hearer to clearly visualize it within his or her mind's eye. Your vision represents what you want to become.

In this sense, there's nothing mystical or vague about a vision. While it should be large enough to inspire you, it also needs to be small enough for you to take actionable steps. At the same time, it must be specific enough to provide real guidance, yet open enough to encourage creative approaches and to remain relevant under a variety of conditions.

A vision is usually considered good or appropriate if it passes both *desirability* and *feasibility* tests. If the future state described in your vision benefits you in a way you find attractive, then it is desirable. Your vision is considered feasible if you have a strategy that explains how it is reasonably possible to eventually achieve the desired state. Conversely, a vision is considered bad if it ignores your interests and needs, or is perceived as strategically impossible.

While the possibility of achievement is important, it is also perfectly acceptable in some cases for a vision to eternally remain just out of reach. In this case, however — creating your vision of the rewards of a successful college career — it is essential that your vision be seen as attainable, even though its achievement may (and should) require your best efforts.

To summarize, your vision statement is a collection of concise, succinct and carefully chosen words that describe a graphic picture of the *future* you. It articulates, "I *am* this and have *attained* that!"

Here are a few examples of vision statements created by students just beginning their college education:

"To be recognized by the medical community as one of the top pediatricians in the country."

"To win a Newberry Award and be recognized as one of the best-selling children's book authors in America."

"To own a national chain of successful dog grooming franchises, grossing over $2 million annually."

Once the functionality of a personal vision statement is understood, it becomes much easier to grasp the concept of strategic planning. A strategic plan is simply a systematic process that maps out how you should go about getting from where you are today to the future you've envisioned for yourself. Your vision becomes the target around which specific goals and objectives are created, in order to move you in incremental steps to your desired outcome.

The sooner you create your vision of your post-college life or career, the sooner you will begin making wise choices about such things as which classes to take, what types of people on campus you should get to know and begin to network with, how you might best use your summer vacation, and so on. Having a clear vision will also help you to recognize which opportunities and activities to say no to, because they detract from the achievement of your vision. If you have not yet chosen a field of study or are uncertain about your future career, you can still benefit from creating a vision for yourself six months, a year, or two years into the future. By the end of the specified period of time, what do you want to have become, achieved, or obtained? Remember, be as specific and graphic as possible.

Using visualization to make your vision a reality

Once you have a clear vision of yourself in the future, the techniques of visualization and mental rehearsal can be powerful tools to ensure its achievement.

The success of these techniques is based on the principle that the way we view situations and the self-talk used as we engage in specific activities directly affects our ability to achieve positive results. Visualizing ourselves being successful in the anticipated situation conditions the mind and body to think and perform in the desired way at the desired time. We mentally see ourselves performing successfully and that becomes our self-fulfilling prophecy. Studies have shown this to be one of the key differences in the psychology of a winner and that of a loser. It is also the difference between a straight A student and a C student!

It has been proven that physical skills can be practiced nearly as effectively with mental rehearsal as they can with physical practice; the brain seems to be stimulated in identical ways without using the physical body. During the 1970s, Eastern Block countries began developing techniques in imagery when preparing their athletes for the Olympics. The results of their experiments were dramatic.

Today, visualization and mental rehearsal are routinely used in nearly every performance-related field to supplement more conventional forms of training and to improve performance outcomes. The power of visualization is so strong that is has been found to influence our physiology at a microbiological level. Cancer patients, who were taught to repeatedly visualize their tumors shrinking and cancer cells dying as an adjunct to chemotherapy, got well at a significantly higher rate than a control group receiving only chemotherapy. There are countless other studies that demonstrate beyond a reasonable doubt the effectiveness of visualization in a variety of fields and under many different circumstances.

There are many books available to help you practice visualization and mental rehearsal, and if you wish to study the topic in depth you should search for them. However, here are the basic steps necessary to help you use the technique to reach your personal vision:

1. Find a controlled environment with minimal distractions.

2. Calm your mind. Relax physically and close your eyes. (If you have trouble relaxing, see the technique at the end of this chapter.)

3. See the future you in your mind's eye. Where are you in your graphic picture? What are you doing? Who are you with? What are people saying to you and how are you responding? Be sure to include all of your senses. How do you feel, what do you think, hear, smell or taste? The images must be vivid and detailed, just as if you were watching a movie. Run the movie over and over again in your head while you are quiet and relaxed.

4. Use repeated affirmation to solidify your vision. Whenever you are in a stressful situation that impacts your vision (such as studying for a big exam), or you find yourself fearful of the future or losing confidence in yourself, recall the images and feelings you saw in your vision and you will be reenergized.

If you're new to this type of visualization practice, initially follow these steps to imagine yourself in stress-free situations, such as walking to class or shopping at the grocery store. Once you are comfortable using the techniques, progress to visualizing the future you. Note that these four steps can be used to practice mental rehearsal for any number of situations and skills. For instance, you can use them to help you remain calm when waiting to give a speech in front of a roomful of people, or to even improve your backhand swing in tennis!

Visualization and mental rehearsal, like any new skills, require practice. Try to spend at least 10 to 15 minutes a day working on your visualization skills. Practice at the beginning or end of each day or between classes. Daily use of positive visualization will help you rid yourself of the self-doubting, negative thoughts that enter your mind. Within every human being there is unlimited and untapped potential; visualization is a powerful way to tap into that potential!

A simple relaxation technique

1. Sit in a comfortable and relaxed position with your eyes closed.

2. Take a deep breath in through your nose and hold it briefly, then breathe out thorough your mouth. Your exhalation should be longer than your inhalation. As you breath out, say "relax," or any other word that promotes a peaceful and relaxed feeling for you.

3. As you begin to relax, think about the various parts of your body (legs, shoulders, arms, hands, face) and try to relax all of your muscles.

4. Concentrate on one part of your body at a time and relax as you exhale.

How to benefit from this strategy

1. Create a personal vision statement for your college success.

2. Practice using the visualization technique to help make your vision a reality.

STRATEGY # 5
CRITICALLY EXAMINE YOUR BELIEF BOX

When you change your "stories," you change your life.

In my lectures I often talk about the importance of understanding the Belief Box concept. Understanding the principles involved and acting on them can truly change your life in immeasurable and sometimes miraculous ways. In the next few pages, I'm going to briefly explain this concept and identify some of the implications for your life. However, for this chapter, I want to ask you to make a promise to me and to yourself. The promise is this: Read this chapter closely, taking time to understand the ideas and how they might apply to your own life experience. Then go back and read this chapter a second time. Then read it a *third* time. That's three times I'm asking you to read this. I wouldn't ask you to do this if it weren't important. In fact, this is the only strategy for which I will ask you to do this. I'm asking you to because I know what a difference it can make in your life. Is it a deal? Okay, let's go.

*   *   *

Have you ever wondered how people's perceptions of the world and its events can vary so widely? How is it possible that human beings can share the same planet, culture or community — sometimes even the same household — and have such different beliefs about a single shared experience or event?

There is a story told about three blind men and an elephant. One at a time, each of the blind men approached the elephant and reached out to examine it with his hands, but each one touched a different part of the elephant's body. The first blind man placed his hands on the side of the elephant. When asked to describe what an elephant was like, he compared it to a tall, broad wall. The second man held the same elephant by the trunk. When he was asked to describe it, he noted its prehensile qualities and compared it to a long, thick snake. The last of the three blind men held the elephant by its tail. When he was asked for his description of an elephant, he compared the animal to a thin and somewhat flimsy rope. All three men shared an experience with the same elephant, but their perceptions of its physical reality were very different!

Although each of the blind men interacted with the same elephant, each of them had a different belief about the elephant based on his unique experience with it. This example is only a fictional tale, but it illustrates an important principle about why people believe the different things they do about the world in which we all live.

Our views of the world

The following illustration is helpful in understanding one important way in which human beings learn, and the manner in which each of us forms our unique views of the world.

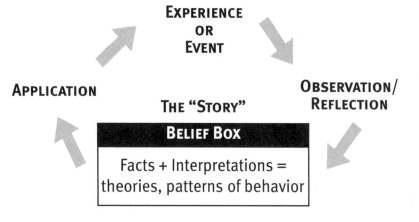

Our unique learning process begins with an experience or event. As we go through the experience, we make numerous mental observations and we subsequently reflect back on what occurred and how it affected us. As a result of these observations and reflections, we create a theory or "story" about what occurred. This story is made up of both *facts* (i.e. those aspects of the experience which undeniably occurred and would be considered true and objectively agreed upon by anyone present at the time) and *interpretations* (our individual, subjective perceptions, opinions and emotional responses based on the facts that occurred).

By way of example, if I meet someone who is 6'2" and I say that he is tall, this is not a fact. It is rather my interpretation of the fact relative to my experience. Since I am 5'10" and most of the men I see in everyday life are about that same height, 6'2" seems tall to me. However, to someone who plays college basketball and associates with people much taller than 5'10" on a daily basis, he might consider the 6'2" fellow to be of average height or even short! So you see that while the facts are the same for everyone, interpretations can vary from person to person.

These stories (i.e., our personal collections of facts and interpretations) become the basis of our subsequent habits, thoughts, and behaviors and constitute our personal Belief Box. We then apply that Belief Box to any similar experiences or events that may occur in the future.

The Belief Boxes in our lives are very powerful because we constantly find ways to reinforce our collection of theories and beliefs. In other words, we tend to pull selectively from our experiences only those aspects that are in agreement with our story. That is, we tend to see only the evidence that supports what we already believe!

For example, the small child who's bitten by a dog and subsequently believes that all dogs bite becomes more convinced of this belief every time he hears that someone else has been bitten. Whenever he hears of another incident, he says to himself, "See, I knew all dogs bite!" The fact that there are many friendly dogs in the world and that the vast majority of them *don't* bite means very little to him because his story, based on his singular experience, is that dogs bite and therefore should be feared!

Stories or theories aren't good or bad, they just are. But as a result of these stories, we adopt a habitual way of doing things and we get locked in. The theories in our lives become permanent.

When people say they "can't do it," or that something is impossible, they are living in the permanence and pervasiveness of their box.

How people get out of the box

When the results we get are making us uncomfortable or unhappy — when we aren't getting the results we *want* — we have to get out of the Box. Sometimes we get out of the Box by choice. At other times, our circumstances become so uncomfortable that we leave our Belief Boxes out of desperation!

There are essentially two ways to get out of the Box. In both instances, the Box is challenged through *unlearning*.

We can get out by:

- *Having different experiences.* These different experiences can be gained by conscious choice or they may occur accidentally. For example, in the previous example of the child who believes all dogs bite, the wise parents might arrange to gradually introduce the child to dogs they know to be docile and friendly, such as the pets of friends and extended family members, so that the child mentally collects a number of positive impressions of dogs and is able to validate through his or her own experience that most dogs don't bite. These new experiences eventually change the child's story about dogs.

- *Going backwards through the observation/reflection stage of the learning process and "reframing" the original experience.* Again, citing the example of the child who is afraid of dogs, he or she, probably with the aid of an adult, might begin to look back at the original negative experience (the dog bite) and ask questions about what happened and why. One possible conclusion might be to realize that the dog didn't bite because dogs are naturally mean; this specific dog attacked because it perceived the child as a threat to its newborn litter of puppies. Thus, reframing looks for other possible interpretations to weaken the existing box of beliefs and to create a stronger and more positive one.

Our personal Belief Box either limits us or empowers us

There is a story told about two shoe salesmen from competing companies. They were both sent to the same remote island in the Pacific to establish a shoe-selling business. After a few short days, the first salesman emailed his superiors with the following message: "Bad news. I've been all over this island and nobody wears shoes! We haven't got a chance here!" Soon thereafter, the second salesman emailed his bosses and wrote: "Great news! I've been all over this island and everybody needs shoes! We've found a goldmine!" Now note that both salesmen were on the same island. Both recognized the same fact: No one on the island owned shoes. The difference is that the first salesman's interpretation of the facts was that he was facing an impossible task, while the second salesman saw the same situation as the opportunity of a lifetime! Both salesmen are facing the same situation, but in the end, which one do you think will be more successful?

The point is that our Belief Boxes either make us feel positive, confident and empowered, or negative, apprehensive and powerless. It depends solely on the way we've chosen to interpret the circumstances or facts in our lives.

Everyone has a Belief Box. Let me tell you a few of the stories in *my* box. I think:

- I'm bad at math;
- I can sleep anywhere;
- I have good health practices; and
- I'm a good writer.

I happen to know where every one of these stories originated. For example, I had a math teacher in junior high school whose confrontational and teasing style of instruction left me feeling incompetent and, at times, even humiliated in her classroom. At the end of the year, I got a D+ in that teacher's class, and as a result I felt that I was stupid at math. There were other ways I could have interpreted the fact that I got a D+, including the possibility that she was an ineffective teacher. But because of the powerful and negative emotions my experience in her class generated in me, the interpretation I chose was "I'm bad at math!"

Ironically, the following year I took a different math class and got an A in the course. But I decided that was a fluke and that the teacher wasn't very smart! Why? Because I already knew I was bad at math! That was many years ago. Since that time, I've successfully demonstrated my ability to handle the math required in my day-to-day life, paying monthly bills, running my own successful business, even serving for several years as the treasurer for a large charitable organization. But to this day, I don't like math because I think I'm bad at it.

In a similar fashion, I also know the basis for the other three stories in my Belief Box. Fortunately, all of the beliefs/stories are not negative; some, such as the belief that I'm a pretty good writer, are positive and are based on positive experiences.

I said that there were two ways to get out of the box: Have new and different experiences so that you create a *new* story, or go back and *reframe* the original experience. But there is also a third way. Sometimes there are no existing facts or evidence to support what you need to accomplish. In these situations, it's necessary to ignore the facts and take a leap of faith into the realm of POSSIBILITY.

You may have seen the movie "Stand and Deliver." The movie tells the true story of a high school in East Los Angeles. The majority of students attending this school came from single parent households. The per capita income was $12,000. Per capita spending in education was $940. The dropout rate was 72 percent and the majority of dropouts ended up on welfare. Based on these facts, what story or interpretation would you create regarding the ability and future of the average student in this school? Certainly not a very positive one.

However, math teacher Jaime Escalante believed that 100 percent of his students could pass the AP Calculus test, despite the fact that he had no facts or history to support that belief. He chose to ignore both the facts of the situation and the conventional interpretations, and instead acted on his belief in an alternative future. If you've seen the movie, you know that he proved himself right. One hundred percent of his students passed the calculus test, even in the face of racial prejudice and unfair testing standards that were arbitrarily imposed on them. This is only one example of the final Belief Box principle: When an unshakable and passionate belief in an alternative future leads to committed action, facts and traditional interpretations can become irrelevant, and results that look like miracles are often achieved!

In summary, we all have Belief Boxes that influence our habits, thoughts, and behaviors on a daily basis. If you're not getting the result you want in a particular aspect of your life, try looking at the facts and interpretations in your Belief Box. To what degree is your story contributing to the undesirable results you're getting? If you can distinguish between the facts and interpretations, you have the power to choose a more empowering interpretation and, potentially, change your results.

How to benefit from this strategy

Think about the Belief Box you have concerning yourself and your abilities. Identify and distinguish between the *facts* and your personal *interpretations* that make up the stories driving those beliefs. Do you have interpretations that are holding you back? How might you go about creating new stories and interpretations that will help you succeed?

STRATEGY # 6
WATCH OUT FOR "MONKEY TRAPS"

I don't care about the cheese. I just want to get out of the trap!

—Spanish proverb

A *young monkey died and went to heaven. As he was waiting outside the pearly gates, he was sobbing and crying so loudly that St. Peter, who was standing at the gate entrance, motioned to the angels to fetch the monkey right away and bring him to the front of the line. When he came face to face with St. Peter, the monkey saw him and began wailing even more loudly. "I shouldn't be here," he sobbed. "I'm much too young to die! Woe is me, oh woe is me!"*

"There, there," said St. Peter, attempting to console him. "I need to take a few notes in my book. Tell me what happened to bring a healthy young monkey like you here so prematurely."

"I...I," stuttered the distraught monkey, "I was just minding my own business and a human clubbed me over the head and... and here I am!"

"Well now," said St. Peter with a furled brow. *"That doesn't sound right to me. After all, you're a very clever monkey. I don't see how a human could just sneak up on you like that. What were you doing?"*

The monkey sniffled loudly, beginning to calm down just a bit. *"Well, actually I had just stuck my hand into a coconut to get some of my favorite food, delicious fresh peanuts, and that's when the human clubbed me!"*

"Peanuts inside a coconut?" said St. Peter. *"Hmmm. Something still seems to be missing. Why don't you tell me the whole story?"*

"W-well," said the monkey, *"It seems that this human got a coconut shell and hollowed it out, see? Then he attached a string to it and put some fresh peanuts inside. He then put the coconut in a clearing and hid behind some bushes. Then like I said, I was coming along, minding my own business, and I smelled the peanuts. I looked around and saw the coconut. When I went to investigate, sure enough, there were the peanuts inside the coconut. So I put my hand inside to get the peanuts. But that devilish human had made the hole just big enough for me to get my empty hand in; once I grabbed a fistful of peanuts, my hand was too big to get out! Then that human started pulling the string and reeling in the coconut with my hand stuck inside. Just imagine!"* The monkey became emotional again. *"I kicked and screamed but I couldn't get away. He must have dragged me 25 or 30 feet. It was awful! And then he clubbed me and... and here I am!"* He began sobbing uncontrollably once more.

"That does sound terrible," nodded St. Peter with great empathy as he closed his book. *"I think I have the whole story now. I can see why you're upset. But there's still one thing I don't quite understand. Why didn't you just let go of the peanuts and pull your hand out?"*

The monkey stopped crying and looked at St. Peter in disbelief. *"What? And give up all those peanuts?"*

* * *

Are you stuck in a monkey trap?

There are potentially many monkey traps in life and, if you watch for them, you will discover more than a few during your college career. It could be an unfulfilling job that you feel is your only option for paying your school tuition. It could be a group of friends who are detrimental to your values and goals but that you've grown accustomed to and are comfortable with. It could be a romantic relationship that you know isn't right for you but you're afraid to lose because someone else may not come along. It could be an attitude or belief you hold on to because it makes you feel safe, feeds your ego, helps you feel in control, etc. Or you may simply be uncomfortable with the prospect of change. There are many possibilities.

The point is there some choices we make that keep us imprisoned for "peanuts."

The next time you are fearful of making a change in your life or routine, ask yourself if you're stuck in a monkey trap. Are you forfeiting your future for what amounts to a handful of peanuts?

Sometimes we have to let go in order to set ourselves free.

How to benefit from this strategy

Answer the following questions:

1. What situations have you experienced in the past that you now realize were monkey traps?

2. What would you do differently in those situations today?

3. How can you apply this knowledge to your present life? How will you use this in the future?

Strategy # 7
Make up your mind to be a class act

Nothing is more important than your reputation.

One of the things you notice immediately when you first enter college is the number of students in your freshman class — certainly far more than were in your high school senior class. Now in this new environment, there are basically two ways you can conduct yourself: You can be a typical or *average* student, or you can be *atypical,* that is, someone who stands out. There are pros and cons to both.

For example, one of the nice things about being typical (i.e., like everyone else) is that you'll have few problems finding friends and fitting in. There will always be people to hang with, goof off with, study with, party with, laugh, cry, etc. These things make you feel safe and secure and can be very important at times. The down side is that you are, as already pointed out, like most everybody else. You're "middle of the pack," not particularly noticeable or memorable.

The other way to go is to be atypical or different. Of course there are various degrees of different, but for the sake of this discussion I mean different in a *positive* way. The major pro is that, again, you're memorable. You stand out and this can pay off in a big way if you spin it right. The con is that being different, even different in a positive or desirable way, can be lonely. You will often find that most typical students don't think the way you think or value the things you value. As a result, even when you're in a crowd, you can feel isolated and alone.

Only you can decide which route you want to take, and since there's a price you pay for either choice, you want to give it some thought and not just let it happen. But while you're thinking, let me give you some advice.

Go for *different*.

You probably expected me to say that. After all, "be an original" has practically become a cliché in our society (although very few people are really true to the spirit of the idea).

But what may surprise you is the reason I am telling you this. As you go through life, what you will discover is that the most important asset you have is your reputation. Is the type of job or career you choose important? In certain situations, yes. Is your annual income important? Again, depending on the situation and what you need to get done, yes. Are your SAT and ACT test scores important? Are your grades important? Is going to graduate school important? If you care where you go to school, if you want to graduate on time, and if you want to increase your employment options, the answers are yes, yes and *yes*!

But nothing is more important than your reputation. Why? Because your reputation will determine how you are perceived by your peers, bosses, teachers, subordinates, in short by society. And if your reputation is gold, people will willingly (often eagerly) find a way to look past any shortcomings you may have in other areas.

Let me give you an example. In high school, did you know anyone who was really smart, got great grades and clearly had an enviable brain, but they were essentially a *jerk?* Did you know any talented athletes who were egotistical to the point of making you nauseous? Do you know anyone now, either personally or in the news, who makes a lot of money but has a reputation for being intensely disliked by their peers or subordinates? When you think about any of these individuals, would you feel inspired to go out of your way to do them a favor or help them in any way?

Probably not.

Now consider once more the really smart classmate mentioned above. Let's say on the one hand you have this super achiever who is also a super jerk, and on the other hand you have someone who perhaps isn't quite as smart but is known to be a hard worker, conscientious, friendly, and easy to get along with. Which of the two do you think is more likely to always be surrounded by loyal friends they can count on? Which do you think will be promoted faster in most companies and organizations? Which do you think teachers and professors will say nice things about and will want to go out of their way to help? Which do you think will ultimately go further in life? Yep, the second one.

Trust me on this. Your reputation is like currency. Do everything in your power to protect it and to increase its value.

Now bear in mind that college is an easy place to ruin a reputation. Being away from home, you have so much more freedom you never had before that it only takes a handful of poor decisions to earn the kind of reputation that could take you years to repair!

Does this mean you have to be dull and boring? Not at all! Go out and have fun, enjoy college to the fullest. But while you're living your life, regularly ask yourself two questions:

1. Are my attitudes and behaviors an accurate reflection of how I'd like to be perceived by the rest of the world (i.e.,

do I act like someone I would want and respect as a friend, a classmate, a student, or an employee)?

2. If the answer to any aspect of the above question is no, what do I need to do differently?

In short, I am suggesting that you make up your mind to be a *class act*. And I'm going to suggest that if you want to be a class act, there are at least 15 qualities or characteristics you should strive to incorporate into your personality and behavior. Please consider each of them carefully because they're all important.

What it means to be a class act

To be a class act means:

• To have integrity

To have integrity means to display a consistency between what you say and what you do. For example, if you publicly tell people you believe using illegal drugs is wrong, then you also don't use illegal drugs in your private life. Conversely, if you did use drugs after publicly denouncing them, you would not have integrity; you would be a hypocrite.

• To be reliable

Reliability means doing what you say you're going to do when you say you're going to do it.

• To be self-disciplined

When you have self-discipline, you do what you know you should do, when you know you should do it, whether you feel like it or not. There is a direct correlation between discipline and self-esteem. The more you discipline yourself to do the things that you know are best for you, the more you like and respect yourself. And the more you like and respect yourself, the more capable you are of disciplining yourself to do things you know you should do.

• To always carry out your responsibilities in a professional manner

To be a professional is an extension of reliability and self-discipline. It means doing what you say you're going to do, when you say you're going to do it, whether you feel like it or not, and still doing it well. Professionals rarely make excuses and they always do a quality job, regardless of their personal circumstances.

Professionals also *look* the part. The college environment is generally a relaxed atmosphere, but it's important to always strive to maintain a relatively neat and clean appearance. Why? Because, fair or unfair, people do judge a book by its cover and first impressions mean a lot. Since you never know how the next person you meet might affect your college career, it pays to always look as well groomed as possible. It's okay (not to mention fun) to be fashionable, but try to avoid going out in public looking like a bum. Just because a particular outfit looks good on your favorite rock star or Hollywood actor, it doesn't mean it's going to look good on you. Wear clothes that compliment you. Mustaches and beards should be well trimmed and cared for, and fingernails should likewise be trimmed and clean. Most women use some type of perfume; you guys might also want to find and use a cologne that you like. And of course, keeping a container of breath mints handy is always a good idea.

If you feel like your overall appearance needs upgrading and you're at a loss as to where to begin, an easy solution is to pick someone you admire and respect and emulate them. Try to find someone who is similar to you in coloring, build, hair type, etc. Then notice what looks good on them and strive to copy it. Although some changes will be inevitable and necessary, this approach will nonetheless give you a good foundation upon which you can build.

Finally, carefully monitor your language and modes of expression. Never use vulgar or "bathroom" language in public and avoid humor based on race, sex, religion, anything off-color, or any type of physical or mental disabilities. You may think making jokes of this type will get you accepted by a particular group of people, but the price you pay in the long run in terms of your reputation and the respect others show you is tremendous. Don't risk it! When I was in school I had a number of acquaintances who were in the habit of using coarse language. The funny thing was that when they did, oftentimes they would turn to me and say, "Sorry, Morris." I thought this was pretty funny as I certainly wasn't any kind of saint, but to *them* it was inappropriate to use that sort of language around me simply because I never used it! It's not a bad reputation to have.

• To respect others

To respect someone means to hold him or her in high or special regard. It is an indication of the degree to which you value that person. Your respect for others is visible in many ways, most notably in the manner in which you treat them. Although a great deal of what is considered respectful behavior is culturally based, there are nonetheless several actions that are universally recognized as showing consideration towards others. For example, how close you stand to someone when speaking to them, and the level of attentiveness and interest you display as they talk, are important ways to convey appreciation and respect. Generally speaking, if you treat people the way you think they would like to be treated, you will most likely convey the appropriate level of respect. And if you're not sure how they would like to be treated, ask! This attitude will also earn you respect in return.

• To show up on time

Being where you say you're going to be, when you say you're going to be there, is considered an indication of reliability. Consistent lateness or a failure to show up as promised can leave others with the impression that you are forgetful, insincere, or hopelessly disorganized. Some people believe that the length of time you keep them waiting is proportionate to the value you place on the relationship, and hence, a further indication of the level of respect you have for them. The simplest solution is to plan your day with the expectation that everything will take a little longer than you think, and to build in extra time to allow for unexpected delays.

• To speak positively about others

Speak positively about your school, your friends, and your professors. Criticizing or otherwise making unkind remarks about others reflects poorly on you and inevitably backfires.

• To be enthusiastic

Enthusiasm is an important academic and social tool. Virtually everyone prefers to be around people who are happy, positive and energetic as opposed to people who are depressed, negative, and full of criticism. An enthusiastic attitude can turn almost any dark and mundane environment into a bright and lively place to be.

But what if you don't feel enthusiastic? There is actually a relatively simple solution in the form of a technique known as the "as if" principle. It comes from the work of Dr. William James, one of the founding fathers of modern psychology. Dr. James spent 50 years researching human psychology. One of his most famous conclusions was the fact that you can have any quality you want in your personality if you *act* as if you already have that quality.

For example, if you want to be patient, ask yourself, "How would a patient person behave in this situation?" Then, make a conscious effort to behave (or act) in that manner. According to Dr. James' research, you will soon begin to feel and *become* patient! If you want to be enthusiastic, start behaving (i.e., adopting the body language and mannerisms) like an enthusiastic person would. In a matter of minutes you'll feel and actually become enthusiastic!

I personally used this technique in college classes and meetings that I found to be dull and boring. I began to act as if I was interested, doing the things and behaving the way an interested person would (such as sitting on the edge of my chair, leaning forward, taking notes, asking questions, etc.), and I actually became interested! Why does this work? Because your mind and body naturally strive to be consistent. Anytime you put conscious and focused energy into changing one, the other will eventually follow in order to be congruent.

The as if principle is a powerful tool that can be applied in a multitude of situations!

• To take pride in everything you do

No matter what role you're playing — student, employee, committee member or hospital volunteer — know that your job is important. Work each day with energy and purpose. Whatever you do, give it your best.

• To always greet others with a warm and friendly demeanor

Smiling is an important part of all social interactions and is the fastest way to build rapport. A smile makes you appear friendly, helpful and positive. Just like the quality of enthusiasm, most people prefer to be around someone who is smiling and pleasant.

• To believe in yourself

Once you know what you want in life and learn how to focus your energy, your potential is unlimited. It stands to reason that you should be your own most enthusiastic supporter. After all, if you don't have confidence in yourself, why should anyone else? At the same time, no one likes an egomaniac; they're boring, obnoxious, and self-obsessed. Instead, simply nurture the quiet inner strength that comes from knowing that you can and will accomplish whatever you set your mind to.

• To remain calm under pressure

To observe someone who is calm and serene when everyone else is in a state of panic is like watching a solid oak tree in the midst of a storm. The tree simply stands in its spot, quiet and still, its roots firmly planted deep in the ground, and waits for the storm to pass. Just to see it is almost a spiritual experience! The ability to remain calm in a crisis comes from knowing that you can and will survive; that regardless of what happens, you will learn and grow from the experience; and out of the conviction that if you're able to remain calm and focus on the problem, you *will* find a way to succeed.

• To strive to bring out the best in others

Do you know a few people who make you feel good just by being around them? If you analyze your interactions with them, chances are you'll discover that they spend a significant amount of time inquiring about *you* (your personal views, feelings, plans, etc.) and offering words of support and encouragement. In this way, they make you feel good about yourself, and in turn you feel good about them. Giving sincere compliments to others and accepting them graciously when they're offered to you are two more important ways to make others feel good. It also encourages them to look for and acknowledge the positive things they see around them and in themselves.

• To enjoy the work you do

When people enjoy the work they do, they tend to be much more positive and enthusiastic than most others around them. As a college student, you should enjoy learning, growing, and discovering more about yourself and what you're capable of accomplishing. Know, also, that what you learn today will not only benefit you, but can be used to benefit others in the future.

• To be true to your values

Values reflect the positive or negative feelings you have about specific ideas or behaviors. They are the principles that make you tick and provide the guidelines by which you choose to live your life. In everyday situations, they determine how you spend your time, energy and money. Among your personal values might be spending time with family, economic security, good health or spiritual happiness. You should know your top five or six values at all times and you should *prioritize* them, i.e., your most important value should be at the top of the list followed by the second most important, and so on. Then, when making choices, ask yourself whether the decision you're contemplating is in alignment with your values. If not, you know it's the wrong decision for you at that time.

Your values will and should change as you grow older. For example, what's most important to you now will almost certainly change if you marry and have children. The important thing is to know what your values are at any given point in your life, and to remain true to them. If you do this, you will be the kind of person who creates positive rather than negative energy, and you will never feel uncomfortable when you look in the mirror.

You will indeed be a class act.

How to benefit from this strategy

Take another look at the 15 characteristics that were identified. Which ones do you think you need to work on? Pick two or three that you want to improve on and make a list of the actions you can take to make these improvements.

PART 2:
Your Habits

---

*The patterns of behavior that create
a magical college life*

STRATEGY # 8
SET PERSONAL GOALS

A goal is a dream with a deadline.

Someone once said, "If you don't know where you're going, you'll wind up somewhere else." In essence, this is why it's important to have goals — goals tell us where we're going.

Goals are valuable because they give direction to our lives and help us to focus our attention and energy. But beyond this, goals are absolutely essential for effective resource management. That's because, in order to successfully manage your resources, you must begin with a clear picture of some desired result or outcome. In other words, you have to know what you want. With this destination clearly in mind, you're then able to choose the tasks and activities that will get you there in the least amount of time and with a minimum amount of waste.

For example, if your goal is to drive from Chicago to New York within 48 hours, taking a detour to Florida isn't just an unwise use of your limited resources; choosing to take the detour will actually prevent you from reaching your destination within the desired timeframe. In this scenario, it's easy to see how having a clear goal in the beginning not only helps you to determine which tasks and activities to pursue, it also helps you to recognize which ones you shouldn't!

In the absence of clear and specific goals, we tend to wander aimlessly, engaging in whatever activity appeals to us at the moment. This kind of mindless wandering can be therapeutic at times, but too much of it can leave you feeling lost, empty and unfulfilled. For most people, having something tangible to show for their time and effort is an important part of their self-esteem and emotional health.

When people aim at nothing in life, that's what they tend to end up with — *nothing*. That's why the surest route to your college success is to begin with clearly defined goals!

Goal Criteria

In simplest terms, a goal is simply a statement of your desired end result. To be of optimum value, your goal(s) should be *SMART*. SMART is an acronym that means:

Specific	It should be clear and well defined. Avoid words like *more, better, good, some*, etc., which are too general. For example, if your goal is to get in shape, specify what you mean by "in shape." Does it mean you want to be able to run a mile in less than 10 minutes, do 10 chin ups, weigh x number of pounds, be able to swim 20 laps, or fit into the jeans you wore last summer? Your goal should be clear and simple enough for a child to understand it.
Measurable	Establish concrete criteria for measuring progress. State the goal in terms of quality and/or quantity.

Acceptable   It should be something you feel positive about and are committed to achieving.

Realistic   Realistic means the goal is achievable in your own mind. Not only must you be willing and able to work on your goal, but the necessary resources must also be available to you, including the belief in yourself. If you've never achieved your goals in the past, then start with an easier one that you know you'll achieve. Then, as you get better at accomplishing your goals, you can set more challenging ones.

Time-specific   You have a specific time to begin working on your goal, and a deadline for achieving it. If you don't establish a deadline for achievement, your goal is more of a dream or wish, rather than a tangible target you're determined to hit.

A simple five-step goal-setting process:

1. *Determine what you want.* This first step is the most important one. What is your desired outcome? Your goal should be tied to a graphic picture and a strong emotional state, and you must be absolutely clear and explicit, otherwise no progress will be made. To do this, see a graphic picture of your outcome in your mind. The image should be vivid, almost like a scene from a movie, and it should be in the present tense, i.e., as if you've already achieved it. What do you see in your graphic picture? What are you doing? Who is with you and what are they saying? What else can you hear, touch, taste or smell in your picture? What emotions are you feeling? Take the time to imagine this as vividly as possible. Then write

53

down what you see and feel, and keep it as a record you can periodically refer back to.

2. *Determine why you want to achieve this goal.* What value does it serve? Once you answer this question, you will have established the driving force for your success. Be sure that the answer to this question is in harmony with your personal values and beliefs.

3. *Determine a specific date for the completion of your goal.* By committing yourself to achieving your goal by a certain date, you are able to better plan your time and thus maximize your efforts.

4. *Determine what you are ready and willing to give up or overcome in order to achieve your goal.* Oftentimes, we fail to achieve our goals simply because we were not emotionally prepared to make the necessary sacrifices or changes in our habits and behaviors to make it happen. If you keep in mind *why* you want your goal, it will give you the incentive you need to persevere and keep moving forward when any difficulties arise.

5. *Create a detailed plan to get you to your desired outcome.* Begin by making sure your goal is SMART. Then, generate a list of steps you might take to reach your goal. Talk with others who've already done something similar to what you've set out to do, and enlist the feedback and ideas of friends or relatives. In creating your plan, your objective is to record specific action steps that are measurable and that will get you to your desired outcome. Once you've identified the key steps, break your overall goal into multiple short-term goals, and set a target date for the completion of each one. Doing this makes even the largest goals less intimidating and more manageable.

The Hungarian psychologist Mihaly Csikszentmihalyi (known as the "Father of Positive Psychology") has scientifically proven that those people who have specific goals to achieve and the means to achieve them are substantially more happy than those that don't. Setting challenging yet achievable goals during your college career will keep you emotionally healthy, focused, and on track for becoming the best that you can be.

How to benefit from this strategy

1. Identify and write down three goals for your first (or next) college semester. Use the SMART method to refine and sharpen them. If this is your first time setting goals in this manner, keep them relatively simple, but make them challenging enough that you must grow or improve in some tangible way in order to achieve them.

2. Use the five-step goal-setting process outlined above.

3. Track your progress until your goals are achieved. If you miss one or more of the original deadlines, determine what prevented you from being successful, then set a new target date for the goal(s).

STRATEGY # 9
DO THE THINGS MOST STUDENTS WON'T DO

It's never crowded along the extra mile.

— Wayne Dyer

Think about the following. In any given college semester:

- Most students will miss at least two or more classes due to oversleeping, hangovers, boredom, belief that the class is unnecessary, etc.

- Most students will turn in at least one class assignment after the deadline.

- Most students will submit one or more assignments with poor grammar, misspelled words, or typos.

- Most students will arrive late for a class at least half a dozen times.

- Most students will never set goals beyond "passing with as little effort as possible."

- Most students will never take the opportunity to introduce themselves to their professors, visit their offices to discuss an assignment or ask for help, or attempt to make a positive impression on them.

This is an easy strategy to explain. The underlying principle is simple: *If you do the things most students won't do, you'll get the things most students don't have.* Thus, one of your primary goals in college should be to *not* be like most students.

If you follow the strategies in this book, you will not be like most of your peers. Most freshmen enter college poorly prepared. They have given only minimum thought to the next four years of their lives, and some even see college as a kind of all-expenses-paid vacation away from home. They begin a four or five year journey and eventually reach the end, never recognizing the *real* value of a college experience.

You see, most college students hate going to class, writing papers, studying for tests, etc. But the truth is that these are the things that will actually give them a better life in the future. They don't understand that the very tasks they view as hassles are the greatest gifts they could possibly have.

For example, a majority of college students have a small voice inside their heads that is constantly talking to them. It says things like:

"Why do I have to do this?"

"It doesn't matter if I miss half the class. She never says anything important in the first 30 minutes anyway."

"I'm too smart to be doing this stuff."

"I can't wait to get this class over with."

"That project's not due until next week. I'll wait until then to work on it."

"Why is this professor so hard on me?"

"This paper I turned in for another class is perfect. Why should I write a whole new one?"

"I'll never be able to do that. It's just too much work."

"No classes this week. I think I'll take a break."

Unfortunately, most of those students listen to the voice and the attitude it represents, and they make bad choices based on it. They don't understand that the things they dislike most about college are the very things that will benefit them most. This is true, not because they're actually going to use all those chemistry equations in the future, or because knowing the names and reigns of all the kings and queens of England will actually get them a better job. It's because exercising the self-discipline to study and complete assignments, not just adequately but *to the best of their ability*, is valuable practice for being able to perform in the future when it really counts.

The manner is which you undertake a task, no matter how small or insignificant you may think it is, defines who you really are and helps create the person you will become in the future. The fact is, you can't settle for minimum effort in your classes time and time again, and still retain the characteristics of a *winner*. It's simply impossible. You must practice good work habits in *everything* you do in order to mold and shape your self-image into that of a successful person. That's why it's essential that you view every task and assignment you're given while in college as a valuable steppingstone to greater challenges and opportunities in the future.

If you develop the qualities of self-discipline, perseverance, and commitment to excellence while in college, you will carry these traits with you into your future career. You will have them for the rest of your life.

But most college students don't understand this.

Make up your mind now not to be an ordinary student. Instead, choose to be an *extraordinary* student. You want to graduate knowing that you just had the most educational, stimulating, and growth-inducing experience of your life, and that you squeezed every bit of benefit you possibly could from the last few years. You don't want to *jog* across home plate without breaking a sweat; you want to *slide in*, feet first and dust flying, screaming "*Geronomo!*" at the top of your lungs, tired and sweaty and maybe even a little bloody, but feeling exhilarated and more alive than you've ever felt before.

Rather than being fearful or uncertain about your future after graduation, you want to feel excited and eager to embark on the rest of your life, because you know that you've prepared well and you now know the meaning of success, self-discipline, and accomplishment. If you follow the strategies in this book, you'll achieve all of this and more.

You won't be like most students.

How to benefit from this strategy

Make a list of the things most students do that are detrimental to their academic success. Then make a list of what you will do differently.

STRATEGY # 10
THINK LIKE YOUR PROFESSORS

Question: How do you catch a squirrel?
Answer: Climb a tree and act like a nut!

Do you know this old riddle about how to catch a squirrel? The essence of the answer is to make yourself more attractive to squirrels! It's a little silly, but it makes sense doesn't it?

That same principle is at the heart of this important college success strategy. In this case, the question is, *"How do you impress a college professor?"* The answer is, *"Go to his/her class and act like a serious student!"*

In Strategy # 9, we discussed the idea that one of your goals in college should be to *not* be like most students. The fact is, if you're like most students, your professors don't know you from any of the hundreds of other students they lecture to each school year. Even though your name is on the class roster, the average professor wouldn't be able to match your face with your name if his or her career depended on it (which, of course, it doesn't)! Now maybe the idea of anonymity appeals to you, but consider this: If your professors can't remember you, they can't and *won't* do anything to help you. You see, professors are only human, just like you and me. And just like you and me, they *will* make the effort to help someone they remember in a *positive* way.

Is this important to you? Absolutely, and here's why.

Imagine that you're a college professor who teaches a particular lecture-oriented class with a student enrollment of 125. At the end of the semester, 123 of the students have test scores and project submissions that give you a pretty good idea of the grade you should give them for the course. As you look over their names, you really can't distinguish one from another. So what do you do? You record the grade they've earned and you're done with that group! The remaining two students, however, you remember quite vividly. Here's what you recall about each of them:

Sue introduced herself to you the first week of class and asked some very thoughtful questions about the course and your expectations of an A student. Throughout the semester, she was consistently one of the first students to arrive for class and she always sat close to the front of the lecture hall. In fact, you can't recall her missing a single class, not even the day before Thanksgiving break. Her two projects were well researched, submitted in plenty of time, neatly typed and contained no spelling or grammatical errors. After the midterm exam, on which she received a solid B, she made an appointment to stop by your office, not to complain about her grade but to ask for help on the questions she missed. During that meeting, you gave her some suggestions on additional reading she could do, and she later sent you a brief note thanking you for your help and commenting on one of the passages she'd read in the material you suggested. She's borderline between a B and an A.

The second student you remember is Matt. Matt isn't easy to forget — that's why you know that he skipped at least four of your classes this semester. Twice during your lectures, he inter-

rupted you to ask a question. On one of those occasions, to avoid falling behind in the material you needed to cover that day, you gave him a brief but thorough answer that, unfortunately, he didn't like. He proceeded to cite an obscure author and asked if you'd read any of his work. When you admitted that you hadn't, he smirked a bit and said that his father had done 15 years of research on the subject " in the business world," and what he was learning in his classes was often "out of touch" with real-world application. Later, when he was unhappy with his midterm exam grade, he came by your office unannounced to express his displeasure and to brandish two books that he felt supported his erroneous answers. When you tried to explain why his sources were irrelevant, he wouldn't budge. You suggested a couple of articles he could read for further clarification, but it was obvious that he wasn't interested. He finally left your office after 45 minutes, clearly unhappy with his unchanged grade and with you. He's also borderline between a B and an A.

Here's my question: Which of the two would you be more inclined to give an A and which one a B?

See? Professors are only human, just like you and me!

If you want to get a competitive edge in your classes, learn to think like your professors. What would *you* look for in an exemplary student? How could they *impress* you – without becoming a nuisance or leaving you with the feeling of insincerity? In short, as a purveyor of knowledge and learning, what would a student need to do to make you remember him or her in a positive way?

Any amount of time you spend brainstorming on this question is time well spent. If you're willing to step just slightly out of your comfort zone, your professors can give you a wealth of invaluable hints and tips to help you succeed in class. And if push comes to shove, you *will* get the benefit of the doubt in those borderline situations.

Remember, when you come to college, you're in *their* world playing by *their* rules. Think like your professors!

How to benefit from this strategy

1. Make a list of things you could do to make yourself memorable, in a positive way, to your professors.

2. Make a second list of the things you will *avoid* doing to ensure that your professors don't get a negative impression of you.

Strategy # 11
Consciously Invite Diversity into Your Life

*The diversity in the human family should be the cause of love
and harmony, as it is in music where many different notes
blend together in the making of a perfect chord.*

— Abdu'l-Bahá

If you grew up in an environment in which you were exposed to people from a wide variety of racial, ethnic and cultural backgrounds, you are quite fortunate indeed. That experience gave you a head start in what has become a critical social skill in modern society: The ability to interact harmoniously with people who are different from you.

On the other hand, if you did not grow up in a multi-racial, multi-cultural environment, your college years, depending on your choice of schools, will probably expose you to more diversity elements that you have ever experienced before

In either case, *welcome to the real world!*

There can be little doubt that nothing is more needed in today's society than an appreciation for the diversity of the human family. Even a superficial review of the stories dominating national and international news will reveal the sad fact that misunderstandings and gross intolerance between different peoples and ideologies are at the root of virtually every major conflict in today's world.

While advancements in transportation, communication, and various other branches of science and technology over the past 100 years have made it a social imperative for all of us to be able to work and coexist peacefully with people from every corner of the globe, much of our society continues to ignore the painful consequences of its abhorrent behavior. It's hard to imagine anything more damaging or more reprehensible than passing on this legacy of hatred, narrow-mindedness, and blatant prejudice to future generations.

Fortunately, you have the power to make a difference. The college students of today are the leaders of society tomorrow. You will marry and raise families, own and operate businesses, and serve in classrooms as teachers and role models. You will enter politics, help to enact laws, deliberate on international affairs, and determine the fortunes and destinies of nations. Your attitudes, values, and behaviors will create the world of tomorrow. You can choose to create a world that is free of racial prejudice and bigotry, one that rejects religious intolerance and embraces cultural diversity — but you must begin now.

It's a big job, but the steps you need to take today are simple and extremely easy. Anything you do to foster greater understanding and appreciation between peoples of different backgrounds will help others to create new and more positive "stories" about races and cultures. Equally important is the fact that your efforts will benefit you personally, both now and in the future, as much as they will help in the greater cause of building a peaceful world.

Here are a few suggestions to help you get started:

- Educate yourself about race and race issues.
- Enroll in or audit a comparative religion course.

- Study the history of minority groups in the U.S. You will gain valuable insights and perspectives as you learn important stories that are frequently overlooked in conventional American history courses.

- The more people you know, the more opportunities you have in life; the more diverse the people are, the more your opportunities increase exponentially! So cast your networking and association net far and wide across racial, religious, and cultural boundaries.

- Read books about people and places that are different from what you're used to.

- Get to know people who are different from you. For example, if you're young, make friendships with people who are older. Whatever your background, get to know others who are of another ethnic or cultural origin.

- Join international clubs and organizations where it's easy and fun to make friendships with people who are different from you.

And finally…

- Don't be afraid of interracial or intercultural dating. Today's society, which is far from colorblind, is nonetheless much more accepting about this issue than even a decade ago. That's because a lot of the prejudice of past generations is being replaced by the first-hand experience of a younger generation, more and more of whom have made lasting friendships and personal relationships across racial "boundaries." So if someone who happens to be of a different race or ethnicity strikes your fancy, don't be afraid to make a move in that direction. Even if it doesn't turn into a long-term relationship, you have very little to lose and quite a bit to gain from the experience. And who knows — you may even meet the guy or girl of your dreams where you might otherwise have never thought to look!

How to benefit from this strategy

Look at the ideas and suggestions above. Add as many other ideas to this list as you can think of. Then commit to carry out the ones that appeal to you or that you know you could incorporate into your life on a regular basis.

Strategy # 12
Protect your health

A man too busy to take care of his health is like a mechanic too busy to take care of his tools.

— Spanish proverb

Motivational speaker Zig Ziglar has given thousands of talks all over the world. A question he would often ask his audiences was whether there was anyone present who owned a thoroughbred racehorse worth a million dollars or more. Of course, no one ever raised a hand. Then he'd ask, "If you did have a thoroughbred worth a million dollars, would you keep him up half the night, letting him drink coffee or booze, smoke cigarettes, and eat junk food?" Of course, this question would make everyone in the audience laugh. Not only do horses not smoke cigarettes or drink coffee or alcohol, but the idea of jeopardizing its health and subsequent performance was insane!

Then Ziglar would ask, "Suppose you had a $10 dog? Would you treat him that way? What about a $5 cat?" After the laughter died down, Ziglar would then point out that most people wouldn't even treat a $5 cat in such a shabby way. And yet, we treat our own billion-dollar bodies that way!

In the case of the million-dollar racehorse, if we did own such an animal, we would undoubtedly try to keep him in a near-perfect environment, probably an air-conditioned barn in the summer and a warm barn in the winter. We'd feed him the best possible food, have the finest veterinarians care for him, and see that he got the most advanced training available to help develop his racing potential. We would do all of this for a million-dollar racehorse, and yet we abuse our billion-dollar bodies.

Now you might ask why anyone might suggest that our bodies are worth a billion dollars. That's a fair question. Let's consider just one aspect of our physical being — the human brain.

According to Tony Buzan, renowned brain authority and creator of the popular *Mind Mapping* technique, the human brain has 100 billion cells. Each of them is connected and interconnected like Christmas tree lights with as many as 20,000 other cells. This means that the possible combinations and permutations of thought available to the average person is a number greater than all the known atoms in the universe!

One result of this is that the brain can process millions of pieces of information *per second* and is capable of remembering everything a person has ever seen or heard. In fact, in an experiment cited by world-renowned neurologist Dr. Ben Carson, it was demonstrated that by placing special electrodes in the parts of the brain associated with memory, an 85-year-old patient was able to perfectly recall and quote verbatim a newspaper article he'd read 50 years earlier!

The brain has enormous reserve capacity as well. There are medical histories of people who lost as much as 90 percent of their brains in accidents and were able to function very effectively with the remaining 10 percent, even getting straight A's in school.

One explanation for this astounding fact might be found in research that has been done by the Brain Institute at Stanford University. According to its studies, the average person uses not 10 percent of their potential as commonly believed but closer to two percent! The average person performs at very low levels of output and performance when compared to their potential!

As an example of this, consider the following. There are more than 600,000 words in the English language, *but the average person uses only about 1,200 in a given day.* About 85 percent of English conversation is carried out using only 2,000 words. Ninety-five percent of conversations are covered by 4,000 words *out of the 600,000 words available!*

Why is word usage so important? Because each word is a thought. The more words you know and can use, the more complex and higher thoughts you can think. Studies show that people with limited vocabularies have limited thinking ability as well. It's been proven that you can dramatically increase a person's intelligence by merely increasing their vocabulary over time. If you learned one new word per day, 365 days per year, considering the fact that each word you learn introduces you to or makes you aware of as many as 10 additional words, in a year or two you would be one of the smartest people in our society!

Taking this even further, did you know that you can know 75 percent of everything there is to know on any given subject? According to Brian Tracy, one of America's leading authorities on the development of human potential and personal effectiveness, it's not hard to do. How? According to Tracy, if you read the three best books on any subject, you will be in the top five percent of the people in the world in your knowledge of that subject! Hard to believe it's that simple, but it is!

Of course, the human brain also has tremendous analytical abilities. Unlike animals that can only react to conditions and situations, we have very large frontal lobes within our brains. These lobes enable us to selectively extract information from the past and the present, analyze it, and then use our conclusions to strategically plot a future course of action. The outcome is that, unlike animals, we're capable of exercising a tremendous amount of control over our environments and circumstances, and hence, we can control the very outcome of our lives!

So I'd say a healthy brain *alone* is worth *at least* a billion dollars. And we haven't even talked about the rest of the body — the biomechanical marvel of the human skeletal system, the perfectly synchronized and harmoniously functioning organs, or the complex system of muscles that gives us strength and mobility. A billion is probably a low estimate!

Here's the point: Your physical body is the most incredible asset/resource you can ever have. There is no problem you can't solve, no obstacle you can't overcome, or goal you can't achieve when you begin tapping into the incredible powers of this amazing tool. You are a *super being* with the potential to function at far higher levels of intelligence, creativity, and physical prowess than you ever have before. You would have to be crazy to risk all of that by abusing it with alcohol, non-prescribed drugs, tobacco, or poor nutrition just for the sake of a cheap thrill or to fit in with the "popular" crowd. There's just no other explanation — you'd have to be CRAZY!

Rather than dwell on the things you *shouldn't* do if you want to achieve peak performance in the classroom, as well as in other areas of your life, let's take a close look at the things you should do:

1. Get adequate sleep. Sleep requirements can vary from person to person, but the average person needs seven to eight hours to function at their best. Most of us, especially when we're young, can get by with significantly less sleep for one night and maybe two, but after that it becomes nearly impossible to function at optimum levels. You may not be aware of it, but all aspects of your life — from driving a car, to studying for an exam, to watching the words that comes out of your mouth — suffer significantly when you don't give your miracle machine, the human body, the proper rest. If at all possible, stick to a regular sleep schedule, going to bed and getting up at about the same time every day, even if you don't have to go to class. If you make this a habit, you'll sleep better and feel better in the morning. If you feel you're not getting adequate sleep, lengthen the time in 15-minute increments until you feel rested in the morning. If you're able to wake up without an alarm clock, feeling refreshed and rested, you're probably getting enough sleep.

2. Exercise regularly. Aerobic exercise is key if you want to maintain high levels of energy and look and feel your best. Choose an activity that brings your heart and respiratory rate up to what is called the "training zone," approximately 140 beats per minute, depending on your age, and keeps it there for 20 to 30 minutes. An exercise session of this type, done three to four times per week, is ideal. Walking two to three miles at a brisk pace, jogging, riding a bicycle (including stationary bikes in the gym), swimming, and tennis are among the many options to choose from. Just make it a regularly scheduled activity. If you supplement your aerobic regimen with light weight training, you'll keep your muscles strong and supple and burn additional body fat, even on your non-exercise days!

Now I know what you're thinking at this point: *"I'm so busy — where will I ever find the time to exercise?"* I hope I've already convinced you that you can't afford *not* to exercise, but just in case I haven't, let me give you something else to think about. *Stress* has been universally identified as one of the biggest killers in modern society. To define it in simplest terms, stress is the way we react internally to the external pressures in our lives. It's the negative reaction we often have when there is a mismatch between the demands in our lives and the reserves we have to meet those demands.

Doctors have identified the negative effects of stress on long-term health, and it's not a desirable picture. Among them are heart disease, memory loss, depression, weakened immunity, weight gain, and even gum disease! Regular exercise has been determined to be one of the most effective weapons for decreasing stress. The primary reason for this is because when you exercise you activate the pituitary gland. The pituitary gland floods the system with endorphins that are over 200 times more powerful than morphine. The net result is that you are on a natural chemical high that dramatically reduces stress and anxiety and lasts for hours after you stop exercising.

The bottom line: Take time to exercise. It really is an irreplaceable elixir for mental and physical health.

3. Eat a balanced diet. Unless you have special needs, you can meet this requirement by concentrating on fresh vegetables, fish, chicken, and whole-grain cereal. Also, be sure to add as much roughage to your diet as possible. If you feel that you may not be getting everything you need in your foods, include a good vitamin or natural food supplement. Some studies suggest that many of today's food sources are deficient in key nutrients, and that supplementing our diets with high-quality vitamins and minerals on a regular basis is essential. Whether this is absolutely true or not, vitamin and mineral supplements are a good insurance policy. In addition, be sure to drink lots of water. Most people need eight eight-ounce glasses of water per day to replace the normal water loss that occurs during the course of daily activities. A healthy supply of water insures that your body is constantly flushing out salts, toxins, waste products, and other residues that can build up in your system and slow you down.

And by the way, *your mom was right about breakfast being the most important meal of the day!* On a typical morning, it's been eight or more hours since your last meal or snack, so your body needs to be refueled in order to function effectively. The brain especially requires the glucose found in food and the glucose from your last meal isn't enough to carry you through the morning. For example, if you skip breakfast and don't eat until lunchtime, you will have gone 13 or more hours with nothing in your system. This forces your body to work extra hard to break down any stored carbohydrates or fat and turn them into a usable form for your brain to function, and if you're tying to concentrate in class under these conditions you're fighting an uphill battle. That's why breakfast is so important for concentration, problem solving, and any type of mental performance. It can also affect your mood. If that's not enough to convince you, numerous studies, including several conducted by the National Weight Control Registry, have proven that eating breakfast helps control weight and reduces the risk of heart disease and cancer.

To insure that you eat breakfast each day, you need to set it as a goal. And like any other goal you must first *recognize its importance*; then, *make a commitment* to do it; and finally *make a plan* to do it. Here are a few ideas to get you started.

- Whole grain and complex carbohydrates such as those found in raisin bran or wheat flakes, combined with fresh fruit and soy or low fat milk, is a healthy way to start the day.
- Yogurt, eggs, and reduced fat cheeses are good sources of protein in the morning.
- Whenever you're on the run, keep a supply of breakfast or protein bars handy.
- Single serving size boxes of cereal, re-sealable packages of dried fruit and nuts, a hard boiled egg, or whole grain crack-

ers are just a few of the healthy choices that are portable and provide lasting energy.

- Finally, remember to go easy on fast foods and pastries; although tempting, they provide relatively little nutritional value and can be counterproductive over the course of the day.

Whatever you choose, eat *something*. If you're used to skipping breakfast, try having it for a week. You'll feel the difference and, hopefully, be convinced to make this important practice a lifelong habit.

4. Eliminate the poisons. These include smoking, alcohol, and any unnecessary drugs or medication. The best thing is to eliminate them from your life entirely. No one intentionally sets out to become a chain smoker, an alcoholic, or a drug addict. It's always an "accident" with negative consequences. So why risk experimenting with any of these? If you really want to protect yourself, you should also consider cutting back on caffeine, salt, sugar and fats. I know it's not easy, especially in college. That's why I said at least cut back — every little bit helps!

5. Strive to eliminate the negative emotions in your life. The more you think or talk about the things that make you angry or unhappy, the more angry and unhappy you become. Negative emotions actually depress your mind and body; they literally tire you out.

Most people have a tendency to condemn and complain when things are not going well. One way to overcome this tendency is by canceling out negative emotions using what's known as the Law of Substitution. The application of this law is based on the fact that virtually all negativity comes from anger, resentment, and blaming other people. Whenever you feel angry or upset for any reason, immediately say to yourself, "Wait — I am responsible for this. I am responsible. *I am responsible.*" You will discover that it's impossible to accept responsibility for every part of your life and to be angry at the same time. The instant you stop blaming others and start accepting responsibility for your circumstances, you will feel a tremendous sense of control and a surge of positive energy. Almost instantly you will feel that you are back in control of your life and your situation. (For more on this technique, see Strategy # 2.)

How to benefit from this strategy

Review the list of five things you should do to protect your health. Set at least one goal in each of these five areas that will improve your physical and/or emotional health. Review strategy # 8 to be sure your goals are SMART and to help you follow through.

Additional Resources

For more information about author and speaker Zig Ziglar, or to purchase any of his books, audio recordings or other products, visit his official website at http://www.zigziglar.com.

For more information about author, personal effectiveness coach and motivational speaker Brian Tracy, visit his official website at http://www.briantracy.com.

Tony Buzan's classic book on Mind Mapping and developing the brain's potential is *Use Both Sides of Your Brain*, available from Plume Books USA Inc. (1991).

Strategy # 13
Help other people get what they want

It is one of the beautiful compensations of this life that no man can sincerely try to help another without helping himself.

— Ralph Waldo Emerson

A big part of life is about relationships — that is, the people you know and regularly interact with. But taking it a step further, it's also about the people you *indirectly* know through the people you *directly* know. In other words, your friends have friends. And *their* friends have friends. And *their* friends have friends, and so on. And you have access to all of them. It's called networking, which is a concept discussed throughout this book.

Here's how the networking concept applies to this strategy. It's human nature to want to help others. You may not believe that after watching the evening news or reading today's newspaper headlines, but it's true. Helping others feels good, and we all like to feel good. When someone approaches us and says, "I wonder if you could do me a favor…" our ears almost always perk up, even if only for a minute. That's because instinctively we *want* to help the person because we know it will make us feel good.

The point is this: If someone asks for your help, and assuming it doesn't involve anything illegal, immoral, or otherwise harmful to others, do what you can to help and do it with a pure motive, expecting nothing in return — at least not in the foreseeable future. By helping others to get what they want, you create a tremendous amount of good will; people will always view you differently if they know you're willing to go the extra mile to help meet their needs. And when the opportunity arises, they will be glad, in fact eager, to return the debt.

Now, if the exact person you helped is never in a position to help you in any particular way, it doesn't matter. Because (and this is simply an unfailing law of the universe) *you cannot do something good for someone else without that good eventually coming back to you.* It may not come back exactly as you expect, but it has to come back just as surely as the planets have to revolve around the sun.

Now here's where it gets really interesting. If you happen to know exactly what you want at that time (i.e., if you've identified specific goals in your life), you will find that "mysterious forces" begin to come into play to help you achieve those goals. *This happens specifically because of your habitual willingness to help others.*

Sometimes it comes about because of the fact that you happen to have a specific goal at the time you help someone else, and that person coincidentally is in a position to help you move one step closer to it. Other times, you may have a goal but not know exactly what you need to make it happen; nonetheless, exactly what you need next suddenly appears just when you need it.

You can't always predict how this happens, and why it happens can't be explained completely — but it happens! And the more people you help, the greater the number of direct and indirect contacts you have who, if asked, can put you in touch with just the right person or persons who can help you when the time comes.

That's why if you help enough people to get what they want, you will eventually get what you want. Once you see this work in your own life, you will have a self-validating experience, and no one will ever be able to shake your belief in this powerful principle. Look for ways to test this idea. You'll be amazed by the results!

How to benefit from this strategy

1. Who do you know right now who could use your help? How could you meet their needs?

2. Remind yourself at the start of each day that you are happy and eager to help anyone you can.

STRATEGY # 14
YOU HAVE TO A-S-K TO G-E-T

You've got to ask. Asking is, in my opinion, the world's most
powerful and neglected secret to success and happiness.

— Percy Ross, self-made millionaire

Not long ago I had the pleasure of meeting Jack Canfield, a professional speaker, author, and co-creator of the wonderful *Chicken Soup for the Soul* series of books. Along with his Chicken Soup co-creator Mark Victor Hanson, Jack has enjoyed unprecedented success with these books that have touched the minds and hearts of literally millions around the world. But it almost didn't happen. Jack explained that they actually had a very difficult time finding anyone who was willing to publish the first Chicken Soup book. In fact, *the manuscript was rejected by 144 publishers* — 144 successful and profitable publishers said the book would never sell! Finally an editor at a small publishing house read the book, loved it, and offered them a contract. The rest, as they say, is history. Since it's inception in 1993, the series has sold more then 90 million books throughout the world. It was named "1994 Book of the Year" by over 20,000 bookstores nationwide. *Time* magazine has called the series "the publishing phenomenon of the century." The series has generated billions in revenue, and for each dollar creat-ed, it has touched the lives of a multitude of people.

Jack says his experience with this book "that almost never was" taught him three important lessons. I'll let you meditate on how they might apply to your college experience!

1. *You have to A-S-K to G-E-T.* If you want something in this world, you can't be afraid to ask for it. Whether it's a job, an introduction to someone who can help you in your career, a date with that special girl or guy who gives you goose bumps, or to have your book manuscript published — if you don't ask, chances are you won't get it. Sure, someone might pick up on your interest and offer you exactly what you're hoping for — but that's not the way to bet! The world just doesn't work that way often enough to justify your waiting around for that kind of good fortune to miraculously fall into your lap! No, in this life, you definitely have to A-S-K to G-E-T.

2. *When the world says "no," you say "next!"* If you have a dream, a dream that you truly believe in and you're pas-sionate about, you have to push on no matter what. Obviously the dream has to have some merit — you have to truly believe that your manuscript is good, that you real-ly can sing, that you do have what it takes to be a pilot or a doctor, or whatever, and you have to be willing and able to accept and objectively consider any constructive feed-back you receive. But if you've done your homework and you know that there's something special within you or in what you've created, then when the so-called experts of the world say "no," you just have to smile, say, "Thank you for your time," and then confidently say to yourself, "Okay, who can I approach next?"

3. *SWSWSWSW* — Jack says this stands for "Some will, some won't, so what, someone's waiting!" It's really a numbers game. When you A-S-K often enough, you'll find that some will say yes and some will say no. You can't let disappointment get you down, because someone, somewhere, is waiting for what you have. You just have to find them.

These aren't just valuable reminders when you're in college, they're valuable lessons for life!

Thanks, Jack!

How to benefit from this strategy

Look at each of the three lessons cited. For each one, imagine and briefly describe at least three possible scenarios in your college life in which following the lesson would make a difference.

Additional Resources

For more information about motivational speaker, trainer and author Jack Canfield, or to purchase any of his books, audio recordings or other products, visit his official website at http://www.jackcanfield.com.

Strategy # 15
Seek Ways to Be of Service to Others

I don't know what your destiny will be, but one thing I do know: That those among you who will be really happy are those who've sought and found a way to serve.

— Albert Schweitzer

According to an old Chinese story, there was once a rich and powerful emperor. He was a kind and benevolent ruler who presided over the most beautiful kingdom in the entire world. The only problem was that no one outside the kingdom ever got to enjoy its beauty, because the kingdom was deep in the Dark Forest and there were no roads that led into the forest. This troubled the emperor, so he decided to build a road that would be the most incredible road ever. It would allow people from all over the world to come and enjoy his perfect kingdom.

Upon completion of the new road, the emperor announced that he was going to hold a huge celebration party. He invited people from all over the world to travel the new road and come and join him in the celebration

As an incentive, he announced that whoever traveled the road the best would receive a million dollar reward. The challenge was well received and thousands of people from all over traveled the road as well as they could. Some drove fancy cars;

some jogged in tuxedos; others crawled on their hands and knees; and still others hovered over the road in hang gliders.

As each individual arrived at the kingdom, the emperor greeted them. "How did you like my new road?" he asked. Each person responded without fail, saying, "It was the most beautiful road I have ever traveled. There were some lovely hills, a smooth pavement, and nice curves. It was perfect, except for the one pile of rock and debris left over from the construction crew. After swerving around that, I noticed no other flaws." The emperor thanked each person and welcomed him or her into the kingdom. He said, "I will be announcing the reward winner later. Please enjoy the party until then."

Hours passed and the crowd became restless. They repeatedly asked, "Who traveled the road the best? Who won the million dollars?" The emperor simply said, "I am not yet ready to announce the best traveler. Please continue enjoying the party."

Finally, as the crowd was completely frustrated, a man stumbled through the kingdom gates. His shirt was torn, his hair was messy, he had blood on his arm, and he was completely exhausted. In his left hand was a burlap sack. The emperor greeted him and asked, "How did you like my new road?" The exhausted man answered, "It is the most beautiful and perfect road I have ever seen."

Asked the emperor, "If it is so perfect, why are you so late?" The man responded, "Well, there was one pile of rock and debris left over from the construction. I decided to move the pile so no one would get hurt. By the way, I found this sack filled with a million dollars under the rocks. It must be yours." The emperor corrected the man, "This sack of money is yours. You win the reward because you traveled the road best. You traveled it best because you made it easier for those coming after you."

* * *

The Beatles sang, "All you need is love." That's a very simplistic philosophy but it's also a very profound one. One side of the equation is that in order to fully live and achieve our potential, we need to be the *recipients* of love. The other equally important half of the equation is that we must also learn how to *express* love.

Finding romantic love and enjoying a long-term partnership or marriage is a tremendous blessing, but there are countless other ways to express and receive love. The common denominator in all of them is the effort we make to be of service to others, to regularly give of ourselves in an unselfish expression of charity and kindness. This isn't just a good idea; it's essential to our development as human beings.

By way of analogy, consider a river. If it doesn't regularly give of itself to the ocean, it becomes stagnant and stale. Similarly, the fruit that remains on the vine soon rots and becomes inedible. In the same way, as human beings we must regularly give of ourselves in order to be nourished and replenished spiritually and emotionally.

If you are like the typical college student, you probably feel that you barely have enough to sustain yourself, much less offer to someone else. But no matter how few resources you think you have (including your time, physical energy, money, and miscellaneous material possessions), you can always share some small part with others in need. Working at a homeless shelter, volunteering as an adult mentor or as a big brother/sister, tutoring a classmate, providing transportation for someone, spending time with an ailing friend, shopping for an elderly person — there are so many ways to serve that all you need to do is open your eyes and be willing.

Kahlil Gibran, the Lebanese artist and poet, wrote that we must give of ourselves, "for to withhold is to perish." As you pursue your perfect college experience, be like the river; find ways to empty yourself in service to others and be assured that you will be replenished.

How to benefit from this strategy

Make a list of the ways you could be of service to people or organizations you know. Determine what you are willing to commit to and set it as a goal. Review strategy # 8 to be sure your goal is SMART and to help you follow through. Consider enlisting a friend to accompany you and share your experience of service.

PART 3:
Essential Training
and Education

The skills and abilities that help create a magical college life

Strategy # 16
Take a speed-reading course

A man only learns in two ways, one by reading, and the other by association with smarter people.

— Will Rogers

I'm sure you've heard the expression "we live in the information age." It's a cliché, but it's true. According to one current study, the amount of knowledge and information in the world doubles every five years. There's just no way the average person will ever be able to satisfy their curiosity regarding all of their interests. It's virtually impossible because there's just too much information available. But you can make some serious progress. In fact, you can become an expert relative to the overwhelming majority of people in the world — if you read.

Speed reading is one of those skills I wish I had acquired prior to attending college. To be able to read a book even twice as fast as you currently do would be fantastic, wouldn't it? Any credible speed-reading course will triple your speed, and many of them will get you reading up to a full page of text in just a few seconds with full comprehension and retention of the information. Think about what this could do to improve your grades. Heck, think what it could do for your *social life*! Can you imagine how much more free time you'd have? Do I need to say more?

Learning to speed read is worth your time. The investment at the front end will pay you massive dividends for the rest of your life. This is a hot tip. Don't pass on this one!

How to benefit from this strategy

Research the speed-reading courses that are available to you, including any that offer a self-study format. Choose one and set a goal to take it. Review strategy # 8 to be sure your goal is SMART and to help you follow through.

STRATEGY # 17
LEARN PUBLIC SPEAKING SKILLS

Make thyself a craftsman in speech for thereby thou shalt gain the upper hand.

I like the above quotation for a couple of reasons. First of all, it's true. A person who can confidently stand in front of a crowd and deliver a persuasive talk is a powerful person indeed. Just look at all the political and business leaders in the world today — most of them got where they are because they were persuasive speakers!

But the other reason I really like it is that it was found inscribed on a 3,000-year-old Egyptian tomb! That means that for literally thousands of years, society has recognized the value of being able to educate, inspire, influence, entertain, and motivate large numbers of people through the spoken word.

No other single skill opens more doors, creates more opportunity, or gives you more power than public speaking. As a college student, you should have more than a few opportunities to make presentations and, if not, you should create your own. It's the perfect way to influence people and leave a memorable impression. And you know what's really great about it? *You don't have to be an outstanding speaker!* Just be *good* and you'll do great! Why? Because most people are so bad at it!

If you do *good* what most people do really poorly, you'll stand out in most crowds, including the vast majority of your college peers and many of your professors! And in the post-college world, when you have the ability to make your boss, department, or company look good through a powerful and professional presentation, they'll *have* to promote you because you'll be too valuable to leave in your present position!

Most colleges and universities offer a course on public speaking. If that's not the case on your campus, or if you can't make room on your schedule, there are lots of public speaking courses available on the outside, both for the beginner and the experienced student.

The good courses cover all the basics and even some advanced skills, including how to overcome the fear of public speaking, delivery (i.e., how to use voice, facial expression, and body movement to enhance your message), how to create and structure an effective presentation, and how to conduct a question and answer session.

Ask around and try to get recommendations from friends or other contacts regarding workshops, trainers or programs that are reputable and have a host of successful graduates. In addition, there are frequently organizations on campus that you can join, such as Toastmasters, where you can study and practice with others who are also interested in improving their presentation skills.

I was lucky. When I was in college at the University of Virginia, I was *duped* into public speaking. A friend of mine "volunteered" me to make a presentation on behalf of a club we both belonged to, in front of an organization known as the Jefferson Society, one of the country's oldest debating societies.

I expected a relatively small audience, but realized I was in trouble when the organization's officers (all four of them!) picked me up right before my scheduled talk and took me to dinner at one of the nicest restaurants in the city. I remember thinking, "Man, these guys are *serious*. I think I'm in trouble!"

The "small audience" turned out to be a loud and raucous crowd of about 60 to 70 people, but at the end of the evening they gave me a standing ovation. As a result, I was hooked on public speaking and I decided then and there that I wanted to become good at it.

Over the years, speaking has taken me all over the world, to such diverse locations as Guam, Brazil, the Leeward and Virgin Islands, Kenya, Uganda, and Holland, to name a few of my favorite trips. I've also met quite a few celebrities and other amazing folks, directly because I had earned the reputation for being a pretty decent speaker.

So, if you want to get some nice free meals, go places you might otherwise never visit, meet some people you probably would never otherwise meet, and in general get more out of life, become a *good* speaker. The study of the craft while in college is time well spent and an outstanding investment in your future.

How to benefit from this strategy

Find and take a public speaking course. Then join Toastmasters or find other venues for practicing your new skills.

STRATEGY # 18
MASTER YOUR TIME

You may delay, but time will not.

— Benjamin Franklin

Of all the skills discussed in this section, I would argue that this one, learning to master the wise use of time, is the most critical to a new college student. That's because everything you're capable of achieving, both in college and in life in general, is dependent on your ability to manage your time. In college there are so many things vying for your attention all at once, and you are virtually free to do whatever you like without having to obtain anyone else's opinion or approval. It's easy to forget that your main purpose for being in college is to get an education. And even then, it's essential to know which subjects to spend the most time on, which projects to tackle first, how to plan effectively, etc. This chapter will give you a very good start on developing your time management skills.

Let me begin by pointing out that the term "time management" is actually a misnomer, because it implies that we can control time; but in actuality we can't. Time is fixed and cannot be changed. Everyone gets 24 hours a day and no more. If you squander your time, you can't get it back and make it up. You can't buy it, store it, save it, or replace it. The five minutes that just went by will never be available to you again.

When someone says they want to get better at managing their time, what they really mean is they want to get better at managing their life. Because time management is really *life management.* It's the core skill around which everything else you do revolves. It's a skill like typing or riding a bicycle — it takes practice and repetition. It's very much like a vehicle, such as a bus, that you can take from where you are to where you want to go. It is the external demonstration of self-discipline. As such, the ability to get your time organized and use it effectively is going to determine nearly everything you accomplish from this moment onward.

Most of us have developed very specific habits with regard to how we use our time. If you're like most high school graduates, you have some good habits and you have some bad ones. Habits, as you undoubtedly know, can be very difficult to break. In order for you to change the way you use your time, you must first *want* to change; you must want to alter your behavior, to better manage your priorities, to become more tough-minded, and to exercise more self-control. Reading all the books and taking all the courses that are available on time management will do little good if the desire to change and improve is absent. Like everything else in this book, it is this desire (or lack of it) that determines your success. *Until* you want to change, little will happen. But *when* you decide to change, you will discover that all you need are a few tools and techniques to effectively manage your time.

Getting started

Good time management begins with clear goals and objectives. That's because specific goals give you something to organize your time and behaviors around; they also help you choose wisely between the various activities available to you. The most common mistake people make in managing their time is that they either lose sight of what they set out to accomplish, or they work fanatically to achieve things they are unclear about, or (worst of all) they do something *well* that need not be done at all! Identifying clear, specific goals from the start will help you avoid all of these critical errors.

If you haven't studied strategy # 8 in this book on goal setting, you may want to stop and read that section before continuing here. If you prefer to keep reading, just be sure to go back and look at that chapter as soon as you finish reading this one, because as you can see, goal setting and time management go hand in hand.

Assuming that you understand the importance of goals in learning to better manage your time, I'm now going to give you five key principles that, if followed, will significantly improve your time management skills. They are:

1. Organize your work environment.
2. Keep a "Master List" and a "Things to Do Today List."
3. Learn to prioritize.
4. Work all the time you're at work.
5. Learn to say no.

Organize your work environment

In order to be productive, it's important to have a neat, clean, and relatively uncluttered workspace. I know a lot of messy people argue about this, saying, "I know where everything is," or "A clean desk is the sign of a sick mind." Maybe these people are effective working in a messy environment, but countless studies have proven that these same people become even more effective when they eliminate the mental distractions that are an inherent part of working in the midst of clutter.

To maintain a neat workspace, follow these four rules:

- Have a specific area that is your official workspace in your room, such as a desk or a tabletop.

- Keep items such as textbooks, handouts, notebooks, magazine articles, etc., filed away and out of sight until you're ready to use them.

- Pull an item out only when you're ready to work on it; when done, remove it from your workspace until you're ready to work on it again.

- Keep a Master List (see next principle).

Keep a Master List and Things to Do Today List

Your Master List is a comprehensive list of all the projects, assignments, readings, etc., you need to do. Your Master List isn't like other lists; you don't put it in your pocket or tuck it away in a desk drawer. This list is most valuable when you keep it in front of you and refer to it often throughout the day, to ensure that you are keeping track of your current tasks and that you are handling the most important ones first. You maintain this Master List by adding new tasks as they arise and crossing off the completed ones. When you're ready to handle one of the tasks on your Master List, pull out the relevant file or other material and complete the work. If you do not complete it in one sitting, note it on your Master List and put the item away until the next time you're ready to work on it. Used in this fashion, the Master List becomes an invaluable tool in helping to keep your workspace neat and uncluttered.

A basic Master List should include the following columns across the top of the page. Then, using a separate row for each new task or project, complete each column working from left to right.

- Date (when task was identified or added to the list)
- Name of task or project
- Due date
- Actual completion date
- Miscellaneous comments

A comprehensive list like this that you're able to easily locate helps you to avoid the disorganization caused by many individual lists, helps you keep track of deadlines, and allows you to view all of your important tasks at one time. A good Master List also prevents tasks from slipping through the cracks, and because you're better organized, decreases your overall stress level.

You should also keep a Things to Do Today List. This is a daily sheet on which you schedule all of the tasks and activities you need to accomplish within the next 24 hours. Each evening, review your Master List and pull from it the items you want/need to accomplish the following day. Write these items on your Things to Do Today List for the following day. In addition to school assignments, this list could include appointments to keep, phone calls to make or any other tasks that are important to you. Just be sure that the emphasis is on schoolwork; otherwise, you may want to maintain a separate to-do list for personal items.

Learn to prioritize

If you're like most college students, you probably have more things that you would like to do in a given period of time than are humanly possible. The first step in time management, after identifying your goals, is to recognize that you can't do everything — at least not well! This means you will have to make choices; you will have to *prioritize* your tasks and goals.

To prioritize means to determine the relative importance of all the goals or tasks before you, and to put the ones of *greatest significance* at the top of your list to accomplish. There are many different ways to prioritize. You can prioritize based on due date. You can prioritize based on importance, or what will take the greatest amount of time to complete, or what's most difficult. Whatever method you choose, you want to avoid what's known as "to-do list failure." This is the practice of doing the things on your list that are fun, quick, easy or of personal interest, and procrastinating on the tougher, less enjoyable tasks. It's particularly easy to fall into this trap if working this way allows you to check off a lot of items on your list, creating the impression that you are actually getting a lot done. The problem is that the tough tasks never seem to get done and remain on your list until they become critical and therefore even *more* unpleasant. So find a fair way to prioritize and then discipline yourself to follow your plan!

Work all the time you're at work

Distractions are a way of life at college. There's just so many interesting things vying for your attention — and that's okay because college is your opportunity to learn a lot on many different levels. However, when it's time to work — *work!* Don't surf the Internet, answer personal mail, stop to chat with friends, watch television, daydream, etc. The truth is that very often when we say we studied for five hours, we didn't really *study* for five hours, if you know what I mean (and I think you do)! A great deal can be accomplished in 90 minutes of focused study if you really do focus and don't allow yourself to engage in other activities. *If you're going to work, then work.* If you're not going to work, leave your work area and go do something else, then come back when you're ready to buckle down.

Learn to say no

Interruptions are a major cause of workloads that pile up and quickly become unmanageable. Other people will constantly make requests of your time and energy. It's important to help others when you can, but it should be scheduled in and not substituted for the time you should be working. If you are not in control of your priorities, these people will be the ones managing your time and your life rather than you! Again, saying no to others is infinitely easier to do when you have clear goals and objectives and maintain a daily to-do list to keep you on task. Then it's relatively easy to see which activities will help you accomplish your goals and objectives, and which ones will pull you off course. Learning to say no, both to self-generated interruptions and to the interruptions of others, is one of the most important skills in all of time management.

This chapter is brief but it truly is key to your college success. Read through it again and again, then begin implementing the practices outlined. They *will* help you maximize your time and manage your college life much more effectively!

How to benefit from this strategy

1. Follow the instructions provided to:
   - Organize your work environment
   - Create and maintain a Master List
   - Start using a Things to Do Today List

2. Make a habit of prioritizing the items on your daily to-do list each day. Do the most important and/or difficult tasks first.

3. Commit to working all the time you're at work.

4. Get tougher at saying no to both self-generated and outside interruptions that keep you from getting your work done.

Strategy # 19
Improve Your Memory

*Memory is the stepping-stone to thinking, because
without remembering facts, you cannot think, conceptualize,
reason, make decisions, create or contribute.
There is no learning without memory.*

— Harry Lorayne

Most people think that anyone who demonstrates exceptional memory skills is somehow different from everyone else — that their brain functions on a higher level or is wired in some extraordinary way. But research published in the January 2003 issue of *Nature Neuroscience* indicates that the difference actually lies in *how* these people memorize information.

In recent studies, researchers compared the memorization abilities of average people with those of individuals who've become famous for their outstanding memories, as demonstrated at the World Memory Championships. The researchers administered tests requiring the participants to memorize a series of items such as numbers, faces, and snowflake patterns. In analyzing the results, they found that the two groups were comparable in terms of verbal and nonverbal skills and brain structure, as measured by magnetic resonance imaging (MRI). The only difference they discovered was that the group with superior memories used many more areas of the brain involved in memory and locations. Follow-up surveys with the participants revealed that the superior memorizers had all used *mnemonic strategies* to remember things. According to study author Eleanor A. Maguire of the Institute of Neurology at University College London, the test results indicate that superior memory isn't due to superior intelligence or brain structure, but rather to superior memorization strategies!

The good news is that anyone — even the most forgetful of us — can significantly enhance our memories using these same techniques. What specific techniques do they use? They're actually not very complicated, but one does have to put in a bit of work in the beginning to learn them. However, there are a number of simple tricks that are easy to implement and can help you immediately if you're not already doing them. For example:

- *Remembering where you put your keys, notebooks, cell phone, etc.*

  The most painless solution is to train yourself to put such items back in the same place every time you walk in your front door or begin to undress. For example, put your keys, cell phone and wallet in the same dresser drawer every time instead of setting them down on the kitchen counter, the coffee table, by the computer, or wherever you happen to be. In the same manner, it's also helpful to always put your textbooks, binders and other notes in the same place, such as in a box by the bedroom door or in a specific bin on your desk. The end result is that when you're looking for something that you use on a regular basis, if it isn't in your hands or in your pockets, you know exactly where to look.

- *Remembering items on a list such as a shopping list*
  Create a nonsense word using the first letter of each item.

For example, MOPPiT could stand for mayonnaise, oranges, pears, papaya and tomatoes. The nonsensical nature of the word will make it easy for you to recall after you repeat it to yourself a few times.

• *Remembering where your car or bicycle is parked* Awareness is the key! As you walk away, look around the area where you've parked and verbalize to yourself what's unique about the location. For example, your vehicle may be at the corner of Fifth and Blake Street, or next to an unusual storefront that you often pass, or in the parking lot row situated to the immediate left of the entrance to the store you're entering, etc. Take a few moments to lock this information in your mind's eye and your natural memory will recall it when you need it.

• *Remembering what you study*

Frequent feedback is an important part of learning. Rather than attempting to digest large amounts of information at one time, study one chapter or a small "chunk" of data, and then pause to test yourself. This method will help keep your mind from wandering, but more importantly it will reinforce the information in your memory through repetition. To test yourself, make up your own questions or try studying with a friend (or several friends as in the MasterMind Group concept in strategy # 23) and quiz each other after each section of material.

Allow me to introduce you to Harry Lorayne

Many of you have seen me do a memory demonstration as part of my lecture to high school and college students. In the demonstration, I have the audience quickly generate a random list of 20 to 30 items, while a volunteer from the audience records the items on a sheet of paper. Immediately after the list is completed, I proceed to recall the entire list, item by item, from memory. Members of the audience then call out a number and I tell them which item is next to that number on the list. Finally, I end the demonstration by recalling the list one last time — *backwards!* I don't mean to boast, but it's pretty impressive! Want to know how I do it? Here's my personal story.

One day while I was living in Bermuda, I was rummaging though a small bookstore when I came across a book, *How to Develop a Super Power Memory,* by Harry Lorayne. At the time I paid a measly ninety-nine cents for that book. In hindsight, the information it contained was worth a hundred times that amount and has paid major dividends ever since. Using that book, I learned how to remember names, faces, dates, and the definitions of new and unusual words — all flawlessly. I never again needed to carry a shopping list with me to the store if I didn't want to. I can take a shuffled deck of cards and memorize the order in just a matter of minutes. I once even memorized an entire book from cover to cover simply because I liked it! To this day, I still often include a memory demonstration in my college lectures just to show the potential that is locked away in our amazing brains but often goes untapped, simply because we lack the knowledge about how such things can be done. I don't think I need to say much about how this skill could be an indispensable tool for virtually any college student. But also imagine the impact it would have on your social skills. Imagine being able to remember the names and faces of all your classmates and most of the people at a party! What if you could chat with your favorite professors and always recall the names of their spouses and kids? Do you think that would impress folks and make you stand out? Absolutely!

Harry Lorayne does indeed teach a mnemonic technique for remembering things — the same type as described by the research studies cited earlier. It's highly advanced but not difficult to learn at all. This particular book by Lorayne is now out of print and difficult to find. However, if you go to a good search engine like Google and type in the name "Harry Lorayne," you'll find a number of his other books on memory training. You can also visit booksellers on the web such as Amazon.com and look up his books using the author search option. Of course, there are other books and courses to develop the memory and you may want to investigate them and compare. But you won't go wrong if you use the methods and techniques taught by Lorayne.

As Lorayne says, *"There is no learning without memory."* I hope you'll use this strategy. I promise you, you'll be glad you did.

How to benefit from this strategy

Research and study a book or course designed to improve your memory.

Additional Resources

To learn more about Harry Lorayne's books and other products designed to improve your memory, visit his official website at http://www.harrylorayne.com.

Strategy # 20
Apply the "Monkey See, Monkey Do" Principle

Imitation is the sincerest form of flattery.

This is a huge secret of success that saves businesses and independent entrepreneurs incalculable amounts of time and money each year. It will do the same for you as a college student.

The monkey see, monkey do principle simply says don't reinvent the wheel. Whatever you want to do, find someone else who has done it successfully, then imitate him or her. Follow their formula for success in every way, and you will get the same results! For example, if you know a straight-A or near-straight-A student, especially one who's taking courses similar to yours, find out what he or she is doing and then do the same. How do they prepare for class each day? How do they study for tests? How do they go about choosing topics for research papers and what approach do they take in writing them? Learn from the best.

As I've suggested, this principle originally arose out of the business world, where startup companies and fledging entrepreneurs were trying to find the shortest and least costly route to success.

However, this principle applies to almost any field of endeavor. Whatever you want to do, find someone who's doing it at a level you would like to achieve, then study their approach and imitate it!

Experience isn't always the best teacher — the experience of others can be just as instructive and far less painful! If you want to do something you've never done before, the monkey see, monkey do approach, when faithfully applied, is virtually foolproof.

How to benefit from this strategy

1. Choose an area or skill in which you would like to improve.

2. Identify someone who is knowledgeable in that field and who has achieved a level of success that you would like to achieve.

3. Learn all you can about and/or from this individual. Copy their strategies and techniques and watch yourself progress!

STRATEGY # 21
DEVELOP YOUR LISTENING SKILLS

Listening is more than just waiting for your turn to speak.

Listening is at the heart of every positive working relationship, whether it be friend to friend, parent to child, boss to employee, or student to teacher. We know it's even at the heart of every good marriage; statistically the number-one complaint between spouses is poor communication!

Ironically, how to listen is rarely taught to students during the formal education process. The assumption seems to be that effective listening is natural and anyone can do it — but this is far from true.

You've got to be a good listener if you hope to achieve all you're capable of during your college career. From student orientation through graduation commencement, if you don't know how to listen effectively, you'll be at a distinct disadvantage and always a step behind those who've mastered this essential life skill. Fortunately, you can learn to be a good listener. Here are some guidelines.

How to be an effective listener

The following guidelines for effective listening are applicable in both large groups (such as classroom lectures of a dozen or more people) and in one-on-one conversations.

1. *Remove the physical barriers*

Physical barriers create distance and discomfort. Sit as close to the speaker as possible and maintain a direct line of sight. Avoid having anything between you and the speaker, such as a tall person who partially blocks your view, a column, or piece of electronic equipment. In one-on-one situations, a desk tends to communicate a superior-inferior message. One researcher found that only 11 percent of patients are at ease when their doctor sits behind a desk, but 55 percent of the patients are at ease when the desk is removed.

2. *Lean forward*

Your posture indicates your degree of involvement in the conversation. It not only lets the speaker know that you're interested and ready to listen, but it also helps you to focus and remain attentive.

3. *Look at the speaker*

Good eye contact with the speaker ensures that you won't miss any accompanying body language or facial expressions that might be important to your understanding. It also communicates to the speaker that you're paying attention.

4. *Relax*

When people tap their fingers, play with jewelry, or fidget nervously, it gives the impression that they are bored, disinterested, and would rather be someplace else. It's also a distraction that diminishes the speaker's confidence and makes them question the value you place on their comments.

Periodically taking a deep breath and letting it out slowly can help you relax and release any anxiousness you may be feeling.

5. *Stay with the speaker*

Mentally focus on what the person is saying. It's impossible to fully comprehend his or her message if you're thinking about what you're going to say when they're done. It's like playing a game of catch: If you don't watch the ball as it's coming to you, you'll miss it.

6. *Look for comments of value*

As you're listening, repeatedly ask yourself how you can benefit from the information you're hearing. This habit will also help keep you alert and interested.

7. *Make mental reviews and take notes when appropriate*

Periodically take a few seconds to review in your mind what the speaker has said over the past few minutes. By mentally summarizing what you've heard in a few short phrases, you'll significantly improve your listening efficiency.

In addition, note taking will decrease your daydreaming and increase your retention. Studies indicate that the average person retains 20 percent more information if they take written notes as they listen, even if they never go back and review the notes.

8. *Use the "as if" principle*

Occasionally (okay, maybe *often*) you will find yourself struggling to pay attention in a lecture. It can be very easy to lose focus — there are lots of people in the room, the professor really can't see you very well, the professor may have a monotone voice, the topic may be boring to you or may be information you already know, you may be sleepy, you may be distracted by other things on your mind. There are countless reasons why you might find it difficult to pay attention. In these situations, using the as if principle is a powerful solution, especially when you can't remember the listening guidelines already discussed in this chapter!

The as if principle was discussed in strategy # 7, but the gist of it is this: You can have any quality you want in your personality if you act as if you already have that quality. For example, if you want to be patient, ask yourself, "How would a patient person behave in this situation?" Then behave (or act) in that manner. In the case of listening skills, if you find yourself losing focus during a lecture, ask yourself, "How would a person who was really interested in this lecture behave?" As mentioned earlier in this book, I have personally used this technique in college lectures and meetings that I thought were boring. I began to *act* as if I was interested, doing the things and behaving the way an interested person would (such as sitting on the edge of my chair, leaning forward, taking notes, asking questions, etc.), and I actually became interested! Again, the same behaviors and techniques already discussed in this chapter are the behaviors you're going for, but sometimes generating a mental image using the as if principle is helpful.

The listening guidelines below are specifically for small groups (such as labs, study groups or club meetings) and one-on-one conversations.

1. *Use encouraging nonverbals*

Speakers need to know that you're actually listening. Positive, audible sounds such as "Uh-huh… yes… I see," are subtle ways to convey that you are following along and want them to continue.

2. *Ask questions*

Asking relevant questions communicates that you're pay-ing attention and that you care about what the other per-son is saying. You also stay much more alert as a listener when you're asking questions. Occasionally the speaker in a large group or lecture setting will give permission to the audience to ask questions at any time. Take advantage of this, but be careful not to dominate the discussion by asking more than your share of questions.

3. *Refrain from interrupting and withhold your judgment*
In our society, it's become common practice to interrupt others when they're speaking. We tend to hear just a few words and then jump in with our response. This habit is both disrespectful and conveys that we're more interest-ed in what we have to say than we are in the other per-son's comments. Listen with an open mind and withhold your evaluation until your understanding is complete. Most importantly, don't allow yourself to become defen-sive if you don't agree. Instead, try to understand why the speaker has a different perspective. Again, if you're mental-ly judging what the other person is saying, it's very diffi-cult to fully comprehend his or her message.

4. *Listen for both facts and feelings, and demonstrate empathy*
It's important to listen for facts and key points. But if you want to score major points with the speaker, be sure to lis-ten for and respond to their emotions before you respond to the facts. For example, if a child says, "I don't want to go to the doctor because he's going to give me a shot," the wise parent deals with his feelings first. The mother or father will say something like, "Needles can be a little scary sometimes, can't they?" Notice that they don't immediately try to reassure the child with a firm statement such as,

119

"You're too old to be afraid of doctors." That's because if they ignore his feelings, the child will think no one heard the real message he was sending.

5. *Check for understanding*

When you check for understanding, you let the speaker know that you were listening and accurately understood what was said. The best way to do this is to restate to the person what you've heard, either verbatim or by paraphrasing the message in your own words. This verifies the accuracy of your understanding, and gives the speaker the opportunity to clarify or correct any possible confusion.

In addition, when you take the time to check for understanding, it's one more way to communicate that you believe the other person is important, and that you value his or her message. This will make the speaker feel good and further strengthen your relationship with them.

One of the great things about improving your listening skills is that you can practice at almost any time, in both formal and informal situations. Effective listening skills are essential to learning, and learning is at the core of a magical college life!

How to benefit from this strategy

Review the list of effective listening guidelines. Put them on an index card and carry it with you. When the opportunity arises, place the card where you can see it and practice the techniques until they become second nature to you.

STRATEGY # 22
PRACTICE FISCAL RESPONSIBILITY

You will never regret staying physically fit and you'll never regret saving money.

— Adam Carroll and Chad Carden, *Winning the Money Game*

Many of you will have acquired good money management habits by the time you enter college. Others of you will not have done so. And still others of you will have acquired *bad* money management habits. If you're wondering what the difference is between not developing good financial habits and developing bad habits, it's similar to the difference between eating a bland meal and eating one that makes you sick to your stomach. While the bland meal isn't ideal, it's considerably better than the one that makes you retch! However, the difference when it comes to financial habits is even bigger and it's this: As you grow older and take on greater responsibility for yourself and others, the lack of good habits eventually becomes commensurate with bad ones! Why? Because our society encourages and makes it easy for people to use credit cards and go into debt. Without good money management skills, you soon find yourself in a financial hole that will take you a very long time to crawl out of, and the entire time you're trying to crawl out you'll be pretty miserable! The point is that habits are hard to break, so if you've developed bad financial management habits or no habits at all up to this point, you need to make a concerted effort to get better now, before you have a fulltime job and you are supporting yourself and maybe a few others, too. On the other hand, if you're already supporting yourself and/or others, read this chapter *fast* and begin immediately to practice the essential strategies outlined!

First of all, just what is "fiscal responsibility?"

According to the dictionary, *fiscal* means "of or relating to financial matters." And of course, to be *responsible* means to have moral, legal, or mental accountability; it denotes reliability and trustworthiness. So to practice fiscal responsibility is to take responsibility for effectively managing your financial resources (i.e., money), such as paying debts on time, not living beyond your means, and being financially prepared for the unexpected. For some people, this is a tall order and requires extreme amounts of self-discipline. Generally speaking, these are people who did not acquire good money management habits when they were young and now find it increasingly difficult to break their bad habits.

There are many books you can read on this subject, some of them aimed specifically at young adults, such as the book by my friend Sanyika Calloway Boyce titled *Crack da Code*, or *Winning the Money Game* by Adam Carroll and Chad Carden. These will help you tremendously. To get you started now, however, here are the minimum strategies you should put into place:

1. *Create a budget and stick with it*
   Break down your expenses on a weekly or monthly basis, and figure out how much you can afford to spend in each area. Then stick with your plan. You can do this on a percentage basis or on an actual dollar basis. Using a per-

centage basis is good if the amount you have available each week or month varies, whereas using actual dollar amounts is good if you have a set amount coming in regularly. Don't allow yourself to step over the boundaries you've set for yourself.

One fairly painless way to do this is to take several envelopes and mark them, one for each of your expense categories. For example, your major expense categories might be:

- Food/groceries
- Clothing
- Books
- Entertainment
- Transportation
- Savings
- Charity

Using the envelope method, you would mark a separate envelope for each category. Then each time you receive income, put the predetermined amounts into each envelope, such as $50 for groceries, $5 for entertainment, $3 for charity, etc. This becomes a mini savings account for you. If you have enough in the entertainment envelope for a movie, you can go; if you don't have enough, you postpone the movie until you've saved enough. If you want to eat out at a fine French restaurant but only have fast food money saved up, you either go the fast food route or you eat in your room for another week or two until you've saved enough to go to the nice restaurant. Get it?

2. *Don't spend all you have*

Never leave yourself totally penniless. If you use the envelope method described above, you should always have some savings for an emergency.

3. *Set a little money aside on a regular basis — just in case!*

   Emergencies happen and, of course, they can't be predicted. But you can prepare for the possibility by setting aside a little money on a regular basis. Wherever you keep this money, be sure it is easily accessible to you and not tied up where you can't get to it, such as in a certificate of deposit. If you feel like you have enough extra money that you want to open a CD, that's okay, but be sure you keep this money separate from your emergency funds.

4. *Try to pay your day-to-day expenses with cash*

   Avoid credit cards as much as possible. In fact, unless you have a very unusual situation (or mom and dad are totally footing the bill), I'd suggest you not have a credit card at all in college. If credit cards are necessary or unavoidable, pay off the balance each month. Otherwise, you will be paying significant amounts in interest!

5. *Give a little to help others on a regular basis*

   If you're able to attend college, you are among the very fortunate. To whatever extent you are able, endeavor to make a regular contribution of some sort that will benefit others less fortunate. Make a habit of giving back a little to your church, a favorite charity, a homeless shelter — choose what you think is important. If you can't spare even a small amount of money, contribute your time on some type of regular basis. Whatever you do, the important thing is that you do it in the spirit of helping others. You'll be amazed at the way you are repaid for your charitable actions; it always comes back to you. As mentioned earlier, it has to — it's a law of the universe.

How to benefit from this strategy

Set up a budget and commit to the five strategies outlined in this chapter.

PART 4:
Your Environment

---

*The people and personal relationships that support
your magical college life*

Strategy # 23
Form a MasterMind Group

Keep away from people who try to belittle your ambitions.
Small people always do that, but the really great make you feel
that you, too, can become great.

— Mark Twain

Read the above quotation again. It's true. Have you ever noticed that successful people tend to have friends and work with others who are successful? This is no coincidence. When you surround yourself with people who are committed to personal excellence, you adopt their thinking, beliefs, and attitudes. If you want outstanding results, start hanging out with people who are either getting them or are in hot pursuit! This is the spirit behind the MasterMind Group concept.

The value of a MasterMind Group

The concept of the MasterMind Group was formally introduced by Napoleon Hill in the early 1900s. In his classic book *Think and Grow Rich*, he described the Mastermind principle as "the harmonious alliance of two or more minds that create a friendly environment to gather, classify and organize new information for fast and effective implementation."

A MasterMind Group is essentially a small, handpicked group of people who come together to assist each other to achieve success. Perhaps its biggest advantage is that the group helps its members to *think differently*; that is, to find solutions to problems using creative thinking that might never occur to the individuals if they were working alone. In this sense, the MasterMind Group is the perfect embodiment of the oft-repeated adage "the whole is greater than the sum of its individual parts." Participants in a MasterMind Group raise the bar by challenging one another to create and implement goals, brainstorm ideas, and support each other with complete honesty, respect, and commitment. Because of this synergistic relationship, MasterMind Groups are mutually beneficial to all its members — while someone is helping you reach your goals, you're doing the same for others.

Forming a MasterMind Group

Your MasterMind Group could serve many possible purposes, but as a strategy for college success, I suggest you form one that focuses on academic excellence. If this is your primary focus, it's essential that you pick members who are serious and committed to this outcome. Your peers in the group will be expected to give you feedback, help brainstorm new possibilities and strategies, and set up accountability structures that keep you focused and on track. Along these lines, there are a myriad number of ways in which the members can benefit from the group. For example, the members can exchange study strategies, bounce ideas off one another for projects, critique presentations and papers, share insights regarding professors and their courses, or drill each other as part of their preparations for exams. If the right group is formed, they will become a community of supportive colleagues who will brainstorm together to move the group to new and ever-greater heights of success.

To begin, decide in advance how many should be in your group (five to eight is recommended), and how long the members will be asked to commit (e.g., one semester at a time, or for the entire year). Then look for people who you feel will commit to the purposes and standards of the group. It may be helpful if the first member you enlist is someone who can help you identify and approach other potential members. Since this group will focus on studying together to achieve academic success, it might help if most or all of you are pursuing a similar course of study, but this isn't essential, especially in the beginning. Look for highly-motivated people who are willing to ask for help and support, and are willing to offer help and support to other people. Look for people who:

- Have a similar interest or course of study
- Have the desire and inspiration to make this academic year extraordinary
- Want a supportive team of MasterMind partners
- Want to reach or exceed their goals

After your initial group is formed, you may want to add new members, either to replace those who drop out or to expand the group's size and/or collective resources. Before deciding to let any new members join you, it's important to "interview" them to be sure they'll fit into the existing group and that their commitment level is high. Only allow new members into the group with the unanimous consent of the existing members. Some possible questions you might ask of potential members are:

- What is your commitment to being successful in college?
- Do you have a vision or long-term objective(s) for your academic career?
- What are your educational goals?

- When will you find time to participate in the MasterMind Group?

- What do you hope to gain by being a part of this group, and what do you think the group could gain from you?

Even with a screening process such as this, at some point you'll probably be faced with members who say that they're committed but then don't participate, or who fail to follow through on their assignments and thereby lose the group's trust. If members fail to participate up to the agreed-upon standard, the group must be prepared to ask people to leave, and this should be done quickly once the poor behavior becomes obvious. Otherwise, the longer the behavior is overlooked, the greater the long-term damage will be to the energy and enthusiasm of the group.

In sports, it's commonly understood that if you want to play at a higher level, you have to play with other people who are at a higher level. The MasterMind Group concept can help you to raise your game and keep it at a high level throughout your college career.

How to benefit from this strategy

Set a goal to form a MasterMind Group. Review strategy # 8 to be sure your goal is SMART and to help you follow through.

Strategy # 24
Be smart about romance and relationships

Tell me who your friends are and I will tell you who you are.

— Spanish proverb

As discussed in depth in strategy # 23, who you choose to associate with in college will have a tremendous impact on your academic success. However, your peer group may ultimately have an even greater impact on your social and career development. Research conducted a few years ago by Dr. David McClellan at Harvard University demonstrated that after 25 years, the members of your "reference group" will have more of an impact on your success and happiness than any other choice you make in life.

Who is your reference group? These are the people with whom you identify and associate most of the time. Their influence is significant because as human beings we tend to adopt the thinking, beliefs, and attitudes of the people around us. As the saying goes, if you fly with *eagles*, you will think and feel like an eagle. If you associate with *turkeys*, you will think, walk, talk and behave like a turkey! The people whose company you frequent have a profound influence on every part of your life and everything you will accomplish in the future. Therefore, the lesson is to choose your friends *consciously and with care.*

People to avoid

Some people are toxic, plain and simple. Being in their "airspace" is a threat to your academic success and your emotional health. They're very easy to recognize — they bring more stress to your life than they do joy, and they make you feel worse about yourself rather than better.

They have different names, but I think you'll recognize all of them by their trademark behaviors. Do you know any of the following people?

- Dorie the Drainer: Dorie is always unhappy about something. Her proverbial glass is always half empty. She's constantly looking for someone to help her but rarely offers assistance to anyone else, and she seems to thrive on being miserable. *Your* good fortune gives her just one more reason to moan, "Why doesn't anything good ever happen to *me?*"

- Brandon the Blamer: No matter what happens in his life, Brandon can always come up with someone else to blame. It never occurs to him that his choices and behaviors could be the cause of his misfortunes. Of course, if anything good ever *does* happen to him, he takes 100 percent of the credit for being a "self-made" kind of guy!

- Giselle the Gossip: Backbiting is her well-earned reputation; she loves dishing the dirt and she often adds a humorous spin to her juicy tales. Her stories can be entertaining but you know it's wrong to give her an audience, and your conversations with her always leave you feeling guilty and uncomfortable. Worst of all, you often detect her not so subtle efforts to squeeze a bit of private information out of *you*. Think she'll be a pal and keep *your* secrets under wraps?

- Jackie the Jester: Jackie is a master at putting others down or sticking a pin in their balloons if she thinks they're up too high. If you enthusiastically announce, "I aced my chemistry exam," she says, "Yeah, Professor so-and-so is known for giving easy tests." *Ouch — y*ou've just been put down! Jackie is often entertaining and fun to be around; unfortunately, her favorite entertainment consists of making fun of others. If you wear an outfit that makes you look fit and slender, Jackie points out to everyone you meet how your "bulges are hidden," and sometimes even playfully pats you on the rear to make her point! If you act annoyed, she says she was only teasing and accuses you of being over-sensitive or a bad sport.

- Egotistical Elaine: Elaine's not a bad sort, she just thinks she's the center of the universe. She's a non-stop talker and every other sentence out of her mouth is about her — her likes, dislikes, and general assessment of the world and how it affects *her.* She may pretend to be interested in your life or what you think, but it doesn't take her long to work her way back to her favorite subject — herself!

- Luke the Lothario: Luke is a wonderful and engaging date. He's funny, charming, and nice to look at, too. But as soon as another woman enters the room, he suddenly seems to forget that you exist and shamelessly coos and flirts with the new girl like he's campaigning for Casanova of the Year! After the woman leaves, he acts as if nothing's happened, leaving you feeling dazed and unimportant.

- Racist Ryan: Not a bad fellow at first glance, except he can't seem to stop stereotyping others based on their racial, ethnic or cultural background. His everyday conversation is peppered with snide comments and derogatory references to others who are different from him, and he's not above telling a tasteless joke based on those same stereotypes. A comedian? Yes. Funny? No. Dangerous? On multiple levels!

You don't want to be judgmental; after all, no one's perfect and there's a little bit of Brandon the Blamer and Jackie the Jester in most of us. But when someone's personality is *dominated* by these negative behaviors, you have to protect yourself. Remember, *you train your friends how to treat you.* If you tolerate someone's inappropriate behavior, you encourage them to continue. If they have a habit of knocking on your door or phoning you in the wee hours of the morning to complain about their problems or watch your television, they will keep doing so as long as you open the door or answer that phone. They may even think you approve!

If someone is mistreating you or taking advantage of your good nature, generosity, time, etc., you have to either *redefine* the rules of your relationship or *end* it. For some people, simply saying, "I'm not mad at you. I just don't think we have as much in common as we used to…" or "I feel like we've been growing apart for awhile now, don't you?" is enough to move them along. But other people might not get it and may need to be told exactly what it is about their behavior that's troubling you. If he or she is real friend material, they'll want to work things out. Otherwise, you'll have to say "so long" and/or find creative ways to avoid them altogether.

Finally, if you *must* associate with any of these people, keep them at arm's length and monitor their influence on your own attitudes and behavior. If you don't, the long-term impact will be significant.

Romantic possibilities

You will make many new friends during your college years, and you will naturally spend more time with some than with others. Among this select group will be, in all probability, at least one or two people with whom you feel a romantic attraction. There is even a good chance that you will meet the love of your life during your college journey. If this should happen to you, congratulations! Congratulations, first, because there is nothing as energizing or exhilarating as the hopeful prospect of true love; and second, because the college lifestyle will provide you with many opportunities to get to know this person and the true nature of your relationship. I strongly encourage you to take full advantage of this time and to resist the urge to plunge uncontrollably into the seductive abyss of love; that, my friends, is a slippery slope! After all, why do you think they call it *falling* in love? This is not to suggest that you should enter into love half-heartedly or timidly; if that's your attitude, why bother? But it *is* to suggest that you proceed cautiously and with both eyes *wide open*.

For example, nature abhors a vacuum. When human beings are faced with a scarcity of facts, we all have a tendency to fill in the missing information based on our accumulated prejudices and experiences. *Don't make the critical mistake of assuming that anything you don't know about your new love interest must be wonderful and just what you're looking for!* Remember, he/she is another imperfect human being, just like you. If there's a piece of information about this person that's missing and it's important to you (such as details about their past, personal beliefs, current interests, or how they spend their free time), don't assume... *ask!*

Keep in mind that asking questions shouldn't be an uncomfortable or painful experience for either of you. In fact, part of the fun of falling in love is the process of learning more about each other. Asking about hobbies, favorite books or movies, musical tastes or vacation memories are easy ways to begin the journey of getting to know someone new. In any case, your goal should always be to become friends first. If you can do that, you have a solid basis for building a more intimate relationship over time. Participating in this type of conversation will also improve your social skills, and give you the added experience of learning to interactive comfortably with different types of people. And if it doesn't work out quite the way you planned, that's okay, too. After all, you can never have too many friends!

College dating — what to expect

Some people say that dating is more complicated today than in the past. They argue that the expectations for men and women used to be much simpler and were universally understood. Men were expected to be "gentlemen," women were expected to be "ladies," and the roles of each were straightforward and uncomplicated. But today, these same people argue, nothing is straightforward. People's expectations and individual beliefs run the gamut, so much so that many singles feel that *any* behaviors they exhibit on a date are just as likely to create tension as they are to score "great date" points.

For example, if you're a man and you automatically reach for the check in a restaurant, you may score major points with one woman but irritate another. If you're a woman who prefers to pay her own way, some men will be delighted while others may feel insulted or even humiliated.

So goes the debate, and it's a fascinating one. But my guess is that most of you reading this book are a bit savvier than these people give you credit for. After all, you didn't just step out of some sort of time machine from a bygone era. As teens in today's society, you've observed many of these changes and have even helped bring some of them about. You probably know many of the potential pitfalls and have learned a few things, either firsthand or anecdotally, about avoiding them. So I don't want (or feel *qualified*) to give a detailed lecture on this subject. Suffice it to say that in the vast majority of dating situations, it's a good idea to observe the following two principles:

- Talk to your dating partner before the first date and find out what his or her preferences are regarding male/female roles. The other person may have some very definite ideas on the subject or they may not. In either case, asking will send the signal that you care about their feelings and want them to feel at ease. If you're the type of girl who's uncomfortable when a guy pays for everything, then let your prospective date know this in advance and see if he's willing to negotiate who'll pay for what. Don't make a big deal out of it. Just say, "Okay, what if I pay for dinner and you can buy the movie tickets. How does that sound?" Or if you're a guy, you might say, "I guess you could say I'm sort of traditional. I really like helping a girl with her coat and opening doors for her. How do you feel about that kind of thing?" Keep the discussion light and casual, but be direct and say what you mean.

- Be flexible regarding your date's preferences. Even though he or she may have different views on the subject, that doesn't necessarily mean the two of you are incompatible. If you like the person and your discussion feels comfortable, consider doing things their way for at least one date and see how things go. For example, if your partner would prefer to go out with a group of people for your first date, agree to the suggestion without making a fuss. Dating is often a bit of a game, especially in the beginning stages, so relax and be willing to play it their way.

On most college campuses, there seem to be three questions that come up frequently with regard to dating. First, who should initiate the date - the guy or the girl? Second, who should plan the date? And third, who should pay for the date? Let's briefly look at each of these issues.

1. Who should initiate the date?

   In America, as in most other parts of the world, the man usually invites out the woman. However, college campuses tend to be very relaxed and informal when it comes to dating. As a result, in most campus environments it's quite acceptable for a woman to make the first move. Whether male or female, do what feels comfortable to you.

2. Who should plan the date?

   Many couples want to share equally in the decision of where to go on a date. However, a lot of guys still enjoy the more traditionally masculine role of taking the lead in this area, and many women are quite comfortable with this. Once again, pre-date communication is key. Let the other person know your thoughts and work on reaching a mutually-acceptable arrangement.

3. Who should pay for the date?

   Generally speaking, if you're a guy you should expect to pay most of the time. If you prefer to go "Dutch treat" wherein the bill is equally split, just be sure to discuss this in advance and be certain that your date is agreeable. Whatever you do, avoid the uncomfortable and embarrassing scenario of asking a young lady for her half of the bill when it comes time to pay the restaurant tab. Again, a pre-date conversation will prevent this awkward scene.

   If you happen to be a guy who prefers to have a date pay her own way, you shouldn't feel bad. Of course, there are some women who want and expect to be treated lavishly by a man. They enjoy being escorted to expensive places, and look forward to receiving assorted gifts on a regular basis as an indication of a man's interest. If you feel uncomfortable with this as a man, simply don't date that kind of woman! And ladies, if these things are important to you and your new guy doesn't see eye to eye, find someone whose values are in alignment with yours.

Conversely, what should the ladies do if the guy insists on paying for everything during a date and you're uncomfortable? You can either refuse to go out with him again, or you can acquiesce to his wishes and let him pay. The financial advantages of letting him pay are obvious, but there could be a disadvantage. Most notably, some men feel that if they spend money on a woman, she should be willing to repay him through some form of sexual gratification. *Ladies, if you don't keep an eye open for this type of attitude, you're going to walk into an ambush!* This is one situation in which it doesn't pay to be accommodating just to please the other person. Decide how you feel on the subject of physical intimacy, and then be prepared to stand up for your rights. If you get the feeling that your prospective date may have such expectations, let him know up front (preferably over the phone) what your values are and what you will or won't do. If he gets angry or otherwise responds in an ambiguous or noncommittal manner, then cancel the date and don't see him again! The point is, you have the right to remain in complete control on this issue, so don't be pressured into compromising your values.

Whether you're a guy or a girl, whatever you do, don't turn the situation into some kind of tug of war. Calmly state your desires and if the other person can't agree, move on to someone else. People have a right to believe whatever they choose. If you part on good terms, you will still have another potential friend.

First date Do's and Don'ts

Have you met someone new and feel anxious about making a good first impression? Here are some things to keep in mind:

Do

1. Make the other person feel at ease
2. Keep the conversation going
3. Maintain a positive and upbeat disposition
4. Laugh at their jokes
5. Be on time
6. Be yourself
7. Talk about their interests as much or more than your own
8. Be romantic
9. Be confident
10. Thank the other person for the date

Don't

1. Talk about yourself the entire time
2. Be late
3. Talk about past relationships the entire time
4. Chew with your mouth open
5.   Try to be someone you're not
6. Tease or make fun of your date, or his/her beliefs/values
8. Use foul language or tell off-color jokes
8. Pressure your date for sex after they've said no
9. Propose marriage or kids
10. Ask too many personal questions

Some general dating advice:

Stop searching for love

Instead, focus on self-improvement and being of service to

others. Remember, it's not about driving a certain car, wearing the right clothes, or having the perfect body. Be someone who's kind, fun to be with, and basically happy with yourself and your life. Present the best person possible to everyone you meet. Do these things and love will find *you*.

If you're attracted to someone, go for it!

Don't be afraid to approach someone because you think they're "out of your league." If you hesitate for that reason, just remind yourself that if you assume he/she won't be interested in you, that's just your Belief Box talking (see strategy # 5) and an unjustified prejudice on your part. If that's not enough to push you out there, remember those famous words of basketball's great Michael Jordan. When asked why he took so many shots during each game, he replied, "I miss 100 percent of the shots I don't take!"

If you're a jerk, forget about dating

By the time they reach college, most women are used to dealing with jerks. They have a kind of sixth sense that helps them detect jerks from a distance. Many have developed jerk-avoidance strategies that they avidly share with one another when guys aren't around. If you're a jerk or tend to behave like one, word will spread fast. If this is you, you should forget about dating until you change. Period.

A little flirting isn't such a bad idea

Flirting is more about conversation than anything else, and a little friendly small talk never hurt anyone. Women in particular are readily engaged by interesting conversation. As long as you aren't rude, aggressive, or threatening, you should speak to as many members of your target population as possible every day. However, if you are already in a romantic relationship with someone, flirting should be considered inappropriate behavior. It's dishonest to the person on the receiving end, because you may be giving the impression that you're available, and it's a form of infidelity to your significant other.

Take your time

There are lots of books on dating and how to build a lasting relationship. If you find yourself getting serious with someone, you should do a bit of research and read some of them. However, you don't need to read the latest bestseller on relationships to take advantage of some very old but still valuable advice such as don't rush into anything; find opportunities to work together on specific tasks and projects; observe how the other person responds to stress and outside pressures; and look for someone who shows strong character traits of honesty, adaptability, resilience, a sense of humor, and compassion for others. The list of desirable traits goes on, but these are the basics. Even if you don't end up with this person in the long run, these are good personality traits to have in your closest friends. And remember that entering into a sexual relationship with someone should be done only with the *greatest* caution and forethought; an error in judgment in this area will affect not only your life but the lives of many, many others for years to come.

If things don't work out, shake it off and keep moving

You were happy before you met this person and if things don't work out you'll be happy afterwards. Remember, SWSWSWSW (see Strategy # 14)!

How to benefit from this strategy

Make a list of the people and relationships currently in your life. Consider the pros and cons of each one. Are there certain people you would benefit from by spending more time with them? Are there some you should spend less time with? Why? What is your plan to make this happen?

STRATEGY # 25
STAY IN TOUCH WITH FAMILY AND FRIENDS

*To the outside world we all grow old. But not to brothers
and sisters. We know each other as we always were.
We know each other's hearts. We share private family jokes.
We remember family feuds and secrets, family griefs
and joys. We live outside the touch of time.*

— Clara Ortega

As the years of your life go by, you will understand more and more how important relationships are. And of all the relationships you have, family is arguably the most important. However, by family I don't necessarily mean your biological family.

If you have a mother and/or father who loves you, and sisters and brothers who care about you, then you have been blessed and you should do everything within your power to nurture and hold on to those relationships. Even in the best of families there are squabbles, misunderstandings, and sometimes all-out war, but try to see beyond that. At the end of the day, if the love and the sincere motives are there, hold on to those folks by any means necessary. Be there for them just as you know, in your heart of hearts, they will always be there for you.

On the other hand, all of us aren't fortunate enough to come from loving, supportive biological families. Sometimes our "family" is made up of other people who have loved and cared for us and to whom we owe a great deal. And then there are the friends that we've grown up with. Friends from the neighborhood, school, sports teams, social clubs, and other miscellaneous contacts — all people you feel an emotional connection with and with whom you share a common bond that has significant meaning for you.

These people who mean so much to you — don't forget them. You'll make many new friends in college and you'll form new bonds, some of which will endure throughout the rest of your life. But don't entirely disconnect from your past. Stay in touch. The phone call, email, short handwritten note or greeting card, surprise visit or quirky gift — whatever communication vehicle you choose, find ways to stay in touch, and across the miles let them hear you say, "I haven't forgotten you. Even though we're in different worlds at this point in our lives, I remember what you mean to me." You need these people, these relationships, and they need you. As the years go by they will mean even more.

And when times are difficult and you're not sure how you're going to make it, these are the folks who will be in your corner. They are the ones you'll be able to talk, laugh, and cry with, and in them you will find an anchor and a strength and you will be renewed and you will be able to carry on. And all the while, you'll be doing the same things for them.

As you pursue your magical college life, remember your real family and friends. You will have few if any regrets if you stay in touch.

How to benefit from this strategy

Make a list of the people you would like to stay in touch with. Then make a list of some of the ways you will do this.

Final Thoughts

In this book, I've shared with you 25 powerful strategies that I believe can guarantee your success, happiness and personal fulfillment during your college career. I believe every one of them is a gem of immeasurable value *if* you truly understand it and implement it in your life.

You don't have to use all 25 strategies (although I hope you do) in order to be successful. Even just a few — the ones that will best strengthen and shore up your weak areas — can have a tremendous impact. Sometimes it only takes a small change to turn things around.

For example, do you know the difference between a .275 hitter and a .300 hitter in professional baseball? It's just one more hit in 40 times at bat. Yet the salary difference between a .275 and a .300 hitter in the majors is more than *double!* Imagine – just *one more hit* approximately every two weeks or every 14 games, can increase a player's income 100 percent! Gaining that *slight edge* (one more hit in 40 times at bat) makes a big difference!

In a similar fashion, consistently implementing any one of these strategies can give *you* an edge in college. Implementing a half dozen or more can *skyrocket* you!

Finally, if you've read through this book and still have doubts about your potential, let me say that you don't need to believe that you can do this. All you have to believe is that *I know* you can do it. You CAN do it. All you have to do is make the decision to go for it, to refuse to settle for less than your best effort, and you'll be on your way. You can make that decision right now, before you finish the final chapter of this book.

I hope you make that decision. I've never met you but I believe in you. I believe in your potential, and I know that inside of you is a leader and a winner who can't wait to show the world what you're capable of.

There's only one thing left for you to do: *Take action, and make the magic happen!*

ABOUT MORRIS TAYLOR

Professional speaker, author, and "magical motivator" *Morris Taylor* has presented more than 1,300 lectures, seminars, and workshops in a variety of educational and corporate environments. He has thrilled audiences all around the world with his high-energy presentations in such diverse locations as Guam, Holland, Brazil, Kenya, Bermuda, and throughout the U.S. Wherever he travels, students and administrators agree his unique presentation style is a "must-see" for anyone yearning for the motivation to pursue their untapped potential!

A graduate of the University of Virginia, Morris' professional background includes 14 years working at a Fortune 100 company, as well as the operation of his own speaking and training business. Several of his recorded lectures on the topics of education, spirituality, and community building are in international distribution, and he is the author of six books and several self-study programs, including "The Real Secrets of Successful Public Speaking," and "Maximum Productivity Through Successful Time Management."

Mr. Taylor is owner and President of Talisman Training Associates, LLC.

*   *   *

To schedule a keynote presentation or skill-building workshop, order books or other products, or to sign up for Mr. Taylor's newsletter, call toll-free 1-888-235-8681or email
ContactMorris@MorrisTaylor.org

Order Form

Please send me _____ copies of *How to Create a Magical College Life* by Morris Taylor, at a cost of $12.95 each.

Sales Tax: In Illinois, add 6.5% for a total of $13.79 per book

Shipping and handling: Please add $3.00 for the first book and $1.00 for each additional book.

Total payment, including sales tax (if applicable) and shipping/handling: $ _____

Name _____

Address _____

City _____ State _____ Zip _____

Emai address_____

Payment type:

❒ Check or money order enclosed

❒ Credit card (Visa or MasterCard)

    Cardholder's name _____

    Card # _____ V-code _____ Exp. Date _____

❒ Yes, I would like the book(s) autographed to:

_____

_____

_____

Mail with payment to: Talisman Training Associates, LLC
                              P.O. Box 524
                              Round Lake Beach, IL 60073

Phone orders: 1-888-235-8681 (Please have your credit card ready.)